# Perfect Phrases
# for Meetings

## Also available from McGraw-Hill

*Perfect Phrases for Performance Reviews* by Douglas Max and Robert Bacal

*Perfect Phrases for Performance Goals* by Douglas Max and Robert Bacal

*Perfect Solutions for Difficult Employee Situations* by Sid Kemp

*Perfect Phrases for Customer Service* by Robert Bacal

*Perfect Phrases for Business Proposals and Business Plans* by Don Debelak

*Perfect Phrases for Executive Presentations* by Alan Perlman

*Perfect Phrases for Writing Grant Proposals* by Beverly Browning

*Perfect Phrases for Sales and Marketing Copy* by Barry Callen

*Perfect Phrases for Lead Generation* by William Brooks

*Perfect Phrases for the Sales Call* by William Brooks

*Perfect Phrases for the College Application Essay* by Sheila Bender

# Perfect Phrases for Meetings

**Hundreds of Ready-to-Use Phrases to Get Your Message Across and Advance Your Career**

**Don Debelak**

New York   Chicago   San Francisco   Lisbon
London   Madrid   Mexico City   Milan   New Delhi
San Juan   Seoul   Singapore   Sydney   Toronto

*The* **McGraw·Hill** *Companies*

Copyright © 2008 by The McGraw-Hill Companies, Inc. Printed in the United States of America. Except as permitted under the United States Copyright Act of 1976, no part of this publication may be reproduced or distributed in any form or by any means, or stored in a database or retrieval system, without the prior written permission of the publisher.

1 2 3 4 5 6 7 8 9 0 FGR/FGR 0 9 8

ISBN: 13: 978-0-07-154683-6
MHID: 10: 0-07-154683-9

This is a *CWL Publishing Enterprises Book* produced for McGraw-Hill by CWL Publishing Enterprises, Inc., Madison, Wisconsin, www.cwlpub.com.

This publication is designed to provide accurate and authoritative informa- tion in regard to the subject matter covered. It is sold with the understanding that neither the author nor the publisher is engaged in rendering legal, accounting, or other professional services. If legal advice or other expert assis- tance is required, the services of a competent professional person should be sought.
>    —*From a Declaration of Principles jointly adopted by a Committee
>    of the American Bar Association and a Committee of Publishers*

McGraw-Hill books are available at special quantity discounts to use as premiums and sales promotions, or for use in corporate training programs. To contact a representative, please visit the Contact Us pages at www.mhprofessional.com.

# Contents

# Contents

# Contents

# Contents

# Preface

After 30-plus years in business, at all levels and in many types of organizations, I believe that meetings may be the most important venue where people make an impression on their peers, their supervisors, and their direct reports. Being effective at meetings is an important key to increasing your impact throughout the company.

Meetings play a major role in how people perceive you for various reasons. First, you interact with many people in your organization only at meetings. Second, others can judge you and compare you with your peers by how you participate at meetings. Third, your management style and management potential are often judged by how you participate in meetings, lead meetings, and control meetings. If you can star at meetings, whether you are a manager or an entry-level professional, you will improve your standing both within your group and with people throughout the company.

While the book is written with a focus on business meetings, I've found that the same approach and perfect phrases apply at all types of meetings in a wide variety of settings, including PTA and church meetings, meetings of school administrators and teachers, and meetings involving nonprofits and community organizations. Whether in business, another professional setting, or your personal life, the perfect phrase will help you sway a meeting your way and impress people attending the meeting. Improving your performance at meetings can dramatically improve the quality of your business or professional life.

## The Book's Format

The book is divided into four sections. The first two sections are intended for leading a meeting—the first for situations in which you are the highest-ranking person at the meeting and the second for situations in which you are leading a meeting with people of higher rank. The second two sections are for attending a meeting, either as the highest-ranking person or as a peer participant.

This book covers common situations in meetings and then offers phrases depending on your goals, your status, and the type of meeting. I recommend that you first read all of this book to develop an understanding of the philosophy of scoring points for your career through meetings and then, before attending a meeting, that you skim through the relevant chapters to find the phrases that are right for your meeting.

In some situations, the type of meeting makes a difference in the phrases that would be perfect. For that reason, some chapters cover each issue within five contexts:

1. Informational meetings
2. Team-building meetings
3. Problem-solving meetings
4. Request-for-action meetings
5. Task review meetings

# Preface

Some meetings, such as board meetings or all-day meetings, involve people from throughout the organization. These meetings cover many items, one after another. Some activities will be informational, others will focus on solving problems, and still others will be task reviews. I recommend that you treat each activity as a separate meeting and use perfect phrases appropriate for that type of meeting.

The goal of this book is to prepare you with the perfect phrases for any meeting, whatever your role and whatever the type of meeting.

# Acknowledgments

To John Woods of CWL Publishing Enterprises and editor Robert Magnan for their help keeping focused on the target of straightforward effective communication, to Donya Dickerson of McGraw-Hill, who thought this would be a great addition to the Perfect Phrases series, and to Eric Debelak for his help in reviewing the text from the perspective of a recent college graduate.

# Perfect Phrases
# for Meetings

# Part One

## Managing Meetings as a Supervisor

How employees view their supervisor is to a great extent determined by how he or she conducts meetings. A supervisor is judged not only by the content, goal setting, or results of the meetings. More important are the supervisor's "soft skills": the ability to encourage, empower, and motivate his or her employees with the right phrases that encourage them to buy into their supervisor's agenda, needs, and goals. In other words, meetings are where supervisors create productive teams that make their jobs easier.

# Chapter 1
# Opening Remarks

A supervisor may come to meetings with various goals. The supervisor may have a specific action plan to implement, in which case he or she needs subordinates to enthusiastically take on tasks to meet the supervisor's goals. Other times, a supervisor needs to obtain information about a situation, to work with his or her subordinates to respond to a crisis, or to try to improve communications within the team or throughout the organization.

As a supervisor, you will act differently in each type of meeting, and you need to use your opening remarks to quickly make your subordinates not only aware of the topic, but also of how you are approaching the meeting and what type of response you expect from them.

Always start your meeting by welcoming the participants, thanking them for attending, and, if necessary, introducing them or having them introduce themselves. This welcome and any introductions should be brief or you will have trouble re-establishing control.

## Setting the Tone

You want to immediately establish the tone of the meeting so the participants understand how to act. You typically enter a meeting with the following purposes:

- Give direction or specific tasks to your subordinates.
- Disseminate information with some explanation.
- Acquire updates or information from your subordinates.
- Work interactively with a group of your subordinates and possibly their peers from other departments.

Your initial phrases should establish the tone of the meeting and your specific purposes.

### INFORMATIONAL

State the nature of the information and the source.

- I have information from the accounting department about last month's financials that I'd like to share with the group.
- Our East Coast region has been picking up market intelligence about new pricing policies of our prime competitors.
- I've been tracking our production times, comparing them with our targets, and I wanted to share with you trends regarding our profitability.

### TEAM BUILDING

People often perceive team-building meetings as an implication that the group is dysfunctional. Your opening comment should present the meeting as a positive, growth experience rather than as problem-solving exercise, while making it clear that you will be directing the meeting activities.

■ I thought I'd break our routine and try something different today. An associate came across some materials that he thought might be fun for our group. As a bonus, these activities are supposed to help us improve our communication with each other.

■ The company has come up with some new team-building tools that are designed to increase a group's productivity. I know many of you look skeptically at team building, but I felt that this was one that might really be productive.

## PROBLEM SOLVING

You want to present the meeting as a forum for finding a solution, not a finger-pointing exercise. You want to ensure that the participants realize that you will keep the meeting moving forward and not let it go sideways.

■ Many of you are aware of the problem we are having with [state the problem succinctly]. I'm looking for input from all of you to create a solution. While it is easy to point fingers at others, I feel all of us have an opportunity to contribute positively, and that is how we should focus our meeting.

■ The problem of [state the problem] has been dumped in our laps. I feel our group has the experience and expertise to pull together a solution that we can take the lead in implementing. We need everyone's input and buy-in to succeed. So let's get started.

## REQUEST FOR ACTION

You need action from your subordinates and you need to direct them to take action. It is best to start by justifying the action, which might be to meet your own needs or in response to a request by someone else. Your initial remarks should also make it clear there will be little discussion about the merit of the actions you are requesting.

- I feel we have a short-term opportunity to capitalize on [specify the opportunity] if we can move quickly. I've outlined an implementation plan that includes a part for all of you to play. Since time is short, we don't really have the luxury of considering other options, so, unless one of you spots a major error, we will be going with the plan I've outlined.

- I've been asked by top management to address our back-order situation. They have given me an outline of the steps they want implemented immediately. I've worked with [name person] to fill in the gaps from their suggestions and we have prepared an implementation plan that I'll pass out shortly. Look over your assignment and let me know if you have any questions.

## TASK REVIEW

These meetings include progress reports, a presentation of a catch-up plan if any person is behind schedule, and a discussion of upcoming actions and any support needed. If there are any problems with tasks, I have found it best not to try and solve them at a task review meeting, but rather to schedule a problem-solving meeting. Your initial remarks should confine the meeting to a task review and a progress report.

- We are meeting to review the status of our tasks and projects, comparing our projected timetables with the initial plan, our future steps, and any corrective steps we might be taking. If warranted, we will schedule a problem-solving meeting for later.
- This meeting is to give everyone a snapshot view of where our projects stand and to identify projects that need help getting back on track.

## Clarifying Expectations

You want every participant to know exactly what you expect him or her to do at the meeting or as a result of the meeting. It is your job to make this clear. In all the examples below, you will be setting expectations, so you should finish all of your comments on your expectations by soliciting a buy-in from the participants.

- Unless someone has an objection to the expectations, I'll proceed. (Then just wait five to ten seconds for comments.)
- If we can keep to our format and all of us agree to meet these expectations, I think we can end the meeting on schedule. Does anyone have any comments?

### INFORMATIONAL

Typically you don't expect much interaction at an informational meeting, so you should state how you'd like the information to be used.

- This information is just to keep you abreast of some of the latest developments in the company. I don't anticipate it will require any action on your part.
- I suspect that some of you may want to adjust your action plans based on this information. If you do, please drop me a memo or e-mail about any adjustments you are making.

### TEAM BUILDING

Your expectations should revolve around full participation in the exercise. You should acknowledge that participants might be reluctant to participate, but make it clear that they need to overcome their reluctance.

- I know each of you falls into a certain action mode during our meetings. I'm expecting each of you to leave that behavior behind and just follow the instructions for this exercise.
- Leaving our customary roles is always uncomfortable. I appreciate the fact you are willing to leave that comfort zone behind and participate 100 percent in our dialog today without any pre-judgment.

## PROBLEM SOLVING

You have to clarify two items: one, whether you're going with a consensus decision or your decisions, and two, how you expect each participant to contribute during the meeting.

- I'd like to gather information from each of you before I decide what action we should take. Let's go around first and throw out whatever ideas you think we can try. Try to come up with new solutions no one has suggested already. Then we will go around a second time and you can each state which solution you prefer.
- I'd like to end up with a solution we can all buy into. But I don't want to jump to that conclusion before brainstorming some options; hopefully we can come up with a variety of options. Let's brainstorm for about 45 minutes before choosing the three or four you all feel offer the best chance of solving our problem.

## REQUEST FOR ACTION

You should have already set some expectations in your opening statement that you are assigning participants actions they must take. But you should also ask each participant for some detail on how he or she will handle the assignment.

- What I'll give you is an outline of the action I need. I'll need each of you to send me by memo or e-mail a more detailed plan for executing your part by our deadline. Then we will have a timetable by which to judge our progress at our task review meetings.
- Please be absolutely sure you understand your task when we leave the meeting. If you have any concerns about not being able to complete your task in time, let me know by tomorrow and we can sit down and discuss the alternatives. Otherwise, I expect you'll develop and execute a plan to meet our deadline.

## TASK REVIEW

You review tasks first to see if they are on schedule and then take advantage of what the participants know about the organization to see if there are areas where other members of the team can anticipate problems or help the person responsible for the task.

- We need to help each other out in this task review. All of us know different aspects of the organization, so please speak up if you see where this task might run into conflict with others or if you know of resources, including your own help, that can accelerate the task.
- I would like this to be a cooperative meeting where we use all our skills to expedite each task. If you see a problem the task might encounter, speak up. Definitely speak out if you can help the task move ahead or if you have suggestions of other help that can produce a better or faster result.

## Stating the Expected Results

Since you're the boss, you need to make sure meetings are held for a purpose and conducted to produce meaningful results that benefit the organization and your group. So always tell the participants what results you expect from the meeting.

### INFORMATIONAL

Typically you should state, as the result, the benefit to the participants.

- Hopefully we will all be able to use this information to coordinate our plans more effectively with other departments.
- Knowing our financial state should help you understand some of the directives I expect will be coming to us from corporate over the next six months.

### TEAM BUILDING

While the result you want to see is better cooperation among the team members and possibly a better work environment, you still want to state the result in terms of the benefit to the individual employee.

- The result I'm hoping for is that after the meeting we can see how we can enjoy our work environment a little more, and when things go wrong how we can keep our frustration levels down.
- I believe these exercises will help each of us project ourselves to others in a way that will enhance career growth and generate a positive response from others that will make it easier for us to do our everyday tasks.

## PROBLEM SOLVING

In some meetings you are just starting the problem-solving process, other times you are finishing up your action plan, or are in the middle of the problem-solving process. Your remarks should be clear about where in the process you expect to be once the meeting is complete.

- This is our first meeting addressing this issue [be specific]. I expect that we will identify two or three action plans to investigate for solving the problem and by next week we should be able to come back and finalize an action plan.

- This is the last meeting I hope to have addressing this problem. We need to come out of the meeting with a final action plan that we can start implementing in the next ten days.

## REQUEST FOR ACTION

You expect people to know what action to take after the meeting and then to start acting immediately.

- I need for each of you to understand your tasks and keep to the timetable I'll be presenting shortly. Let me know after the meeting if you have any questions about what is expected of you.

- I've brought you together as a group rather than meet with you individually so that you understand each other's assignments and can help rather than hinder one another's efforts. I'd also like each of you after the meeting to e-mail a more specific action plan to your fellow members in order to facilitate cooperation.

## TASK REVIEW

Task reviews should be interactive meetings that help the participants do their tasks more effectively. Again, try to cast the result in terms of the benefit for the participant presenting the review.

- Hopefully each person or group presenting an update will be able to take advantage of the resources of our group in a constructive way to improve their action plan. If any of you receive any input that you will incorporate into your efforts, I'd like you to send the rest of us a short e-mail about the modifications to your action plan.

- As you present your reviews, point out areas where you would like to solicit input from others for new ideas or suggestions for improvement. The meeting is valuable only if each participant receives some help for his or her project.

# Chapter 2
# The Presentation

Y ou may be making a presentation at the meeting or be in charge of a meeting at which others give presentations. Either way you need to take charge and control the meeting, which you can do primarily by clearly communicating so the participants know how to respond. You'll find it is difficult to keep control of a meeting if you don't preview the presentations that others will make and then prepare comments regarding the presentations, the actions you feel are necessary, and the type of interaction you expect from the group.

## Reinforcing Your Take

Since you are the supervisor and the participants are your subordinates, you will have the final say in actions that occur as a result of the meeting. While you don't want to stifle dissent, you can sway people to your view and avoid endless discussion by simply giving your impression of the presentation before it starts. That gives the participants a framework to follow while they listen to the presentation. If the presentation will be given by someone else, you can start with a short statement indicating you have been able to review the data.

- I've had a chance to review the presentation.
- I talked with [name the presenter] before the meeting.
- I asked [name the presenter] to prepare this information for you.

### INFORMATIONAL

Tell the group before the presentation how you feel about the news—good, bad, or somewhere in between—and also how this information will be useful to them.

- I think you'll agree that we must be doing many things right to generate the positive results you'll see. I think you'll all want to build on our momentum by continuing with the same or similar programs over the next six months.
- This information shows some disturbing trends that indicate that we are falling behind. As you hear the information, consider how any assumptions you may have made for your current programs may be impacting these results.

## TEAM BUILDING

Employees often take a dim view of team-building meetings, so you have to present the meeting in a positive light first and then show a real benefit to the group.

- I've talked with people who've had an opportunity to use this program and they said it surpassed all their expectations.
- I've never seen a communications program that has gathered anywhere near the positive feedback as this one.

## PROBLEM SOLVING

The participants will know the nature of the problem when they receive the agenda in advance of the meeting. You need to comment before the presentation about the seriousness of the problem and also on how quickly the problem must be addressed.

- This problem has been a nagging source of problems for our service groups for over six months and it has caused quite a bit of friction among our companies. While we have other, more pressing problems, I'd like to see us put this problem to rest within the next 60 days.
- This quality issue that [name the presenter] will address is causing a loss of confidence in our dealer network that could snowball on us. We are going to need an action plan to present to key stakeholders within ten days.

## REQUEST FOR ACTION

You should have given a justification for the action in your opening remarks and outlined the response you expect from the group, so you have already strongly reinforced your take on the situation. Here you can emphasize how serious the situation is.

- My presentation is brief and has gaps that I would normally fill, but I feel our push to act was so strong that I wanted to pull you all together as soon as possible.
- I've taken the time to add a great deal of information to the presentation to be sure everyone understands the seriousness of the problem and also to help everyone in the group act cooperatively.

## TASK REVIEW

Typically, presenters offer a rosy view of their progress during task reviews. This is a good time to state how you feel the tasks are going, in order to help those responsible avoid a last-minute rush that typically makes a project less effective.

- This project looks like it is becoming back-end-loaded. If it isn't turned around, [name the presenter] might need some help so the last-minute rush doesn't become a panic.
- I'm considering dropping this project and concentrating our efforts on tasks that are on schedule. Otherwise we could end up hurting other key projects while trying to bring this one up to speed.

## Validating the Presentation

You gave your take on the presentation before it started, but when it ends and before you outline your call for action, you want to validate the presentation as being useful. If you feel that others have a different point of view, you want to control their input now, so you can move on to the action phase.

### INFORMATIONAL

You want to minimize the number of comments in an informational meeting. If you know there will be disagreement, you can either address that upfront or ask someone you feel will disagree for short comments after the presentation.

- I know this presentation doesn't include all the supporting information that many of you may want to hear, but I think it is sufficient to let everyone understand the issue. I know specifically that [list likely dissenters] see the situation differently, but I've supported this presentation because I believe it helps us get quickly to an action response.

- I asked [name the presenter] to pull together a series of key facts so that you all can quickly grasp where we are today. I know [name a dissenter] feels differently. If you'd like, you can have two minutes to make your point after the presentation.

### TEAM BUILDING

If any participants are reluctant, you need to reinforce positive points you feel can result from the exercise.

■ What caught my eye immediately is that this process tackles two issues I think we face: how to decrease our communication and reaction time and how to ensure we get group buy-in, or at least group knowledge before anyone of us act.

■ I think the presentation was quite exciting. I know I have a tendency, like most people, to judge others' actions by what I'd like them to be doing without understanding why they feel they ought to be doing something different. Learning a new way to judge others' actions is a valuable skill.

## PROBLEM SOLVING

As a supervisor you always want to be moving forward. Problem-solving meetings can be a step backward if you let them degenerate into finger pointing. You want to concentrate the conversation on solving the problem.

■ This presentation effectively conveys the nature of the problem. I know we all have a lot of additional information about it, and many of you would like to offer reasons for how the problem developed. But I'm hoping to concentrate our time here in the meeting on solving the problem.

■ I know we could all spend time on what caused the problem, and we may want to meet again to determine the causes, so we can prevent the same problems in the future. The question now, though, is what we can do now to solve the problem. The presentation is clear on the nature of the problem; we need to be just as clear in our solution.

## REQUEST FOR ACTION

You are most interested now in ensuring everyone understands what to do and the necessary timing of each action, all while not encouraging much new conversation. You want the participants to feel free to ask any questions necessary to clarify their tasks, but any additional questions or comments beyond this will be detrimental to the meeting.

■ So is there anyone who doesn't understand what he or she needs to do and when he or she needs to finish the task? Later in the meeting, we can discuss anyone's individual problems keeping to the timetable. Let's first just be sure we know what each of us has to do. I'm open to some of you switching assignments if you feel you can better handle another assignment.

■ I normally don't like to assign tasks without some group discussion and buy-in, but the situation we are dealing with doesn't leave time for that. I know some of the assignment deadlines will be very tight for some of you. But I appreciate all the support each of you can offer to deal with this situation.

## TASK REVIEW

Now that you've heard the task reviews, you want to tell the participants again how you view the progress, as you may need to ask for some corrective action or help from some of them. If you are very unhappy with the progress of a task, this is not the time to discuss that; you should let the person responsible know after you review the proposal and before the meeting.

**The Presentation**

- As I said before the presentation, this project looks like it is becoming back-end-loaded and needs a dramatic turn-around.
- Very good job. This project is running on schedule and we all look good.
- This project doesn't look like it's going to meet its goals.

## Setting the Stage for Action

In the opening remarks you touched on future action, both while clarifying your expectations and covering expected results. That was before the presentation and your comments were therefore general. Now the presentation has been made and it is time to focus the meeting on action, both on which action will occur next in the meeting, and also on which action will need to occur after the meeting.

### INFORMATIONAL

Often informational meetings don't require action, but you should still say so in order to avoid confusion. If there are actions you would like to see happen, now is the time to bring them up.

- I believe the information is self-explanatory and we don't need too much discussion, but I will open the floor up for comments in a minute if you have any. The good news is the report is positive and we can continue on our current course.
- This information might have an impact on your programs or might change some of your plans. I'd like each of you to give me a short response here about what changes you expect from this information.

### TEAM BUILDING

In team-building meetings this moment is awkward, moving beyond talking about the team-building experience to actually engaging in it. To encourage reluctant participants, you may need to emphasize the value of the exercise to you and also to the team.

- I know we all have been frustrated at times between slow and mixed responses that we have received from other groups. One of my top priorities is that our group always be responsive, and that requires teamwork and great communication. Rather than evaluating and deciding where our group needs to improve, I thought it would be better to run through some team-building skills.

- Being a good team member requires a lot of hard work. I feel that I have room for improvement in my teamwork skills and I think these exercises will help me and I hope they help you too. We will forget how we currently interact and what our organizational roles are and just follow the guidelines of the exercise.

## PROBLEM SOLVING

At these meetings you need to be sure the focus is on action and not finger pointing. Typically a problem-solving meeting will result in a specific action to be taken now, a plan to come back with a response within a short time, or a combination of both.

- I'm looking for short-term actions that we can decide upon at this meeting, and I'm hoping we can put together a plan for a longer-term solution.

- This is a high-profile problem: I believe we need to show first that we are concerned and second that we are committing a major portion of our resources to addressing this issue. We can't look like we are disregarding the problem. I need all of you to both offer solutions and suggest specific action you can take to help.

## REQUEST FOR ACTION

You don't have to do much about action at these meetings, as you have already called for action in your presentation. Simply ask for an immediate response from the group.

- OK, I'd like each of you to drop me an e-mail tomorrow confirming your action and response date, with a short timetable for your potential actions.
- I'm counting on everyone to do the task assigned. Each of you has a piece of the action plan and I'll be left holding the bag if any of you fail in your tasks. This is a tricky assignment and we will fail if we wait until the last minute to act.

## TASK REVIEW

Here your responses can range from offering kudos to telling the group that you should cancel this project because it's going nowhere. No action is required for projects on schedule, but you need a response for projects that are behind.

- This project is obviously behind schedule. [Name the presenter], I'd like to ask what actions you plan on taking to get back on schedule. The rest of you, I'd like to know who of you can help out and in what capacity. [Name the presenter], I want an honest assessment of whether you can get back on schedule with the help of your teammates and, if not, what additional help you need.
- I can't justify putting time and resources into a project that is so far behind it may never get completed and, even if it does, the group still will look bad for being so late. I'd rather we take our lumps now and then come back and start the project anew in six months or just forget the project forever.

# Chapter 3
# Group Reaction and
# Participation

You can have complete control of the group through the opening and the presentation, but control can easily slip away once the presentation ends. You want to keep the meeting moving toward the objective. You need to keep all the participants focused on the objective, but at the same time you want each of them to feel he or she has an opportunity to offer input and have it considered by the other participants and by the leader. Knowing how to control that flow to keep the proper balance is what makes a supervisor effective.

In this chapter the comments are not split up based on the type of meeting, because controlling participation is the same for all meetings.

## Gathering Opinions from Everyone

In many meetings you want to get opinions from some or all of the participants. But you have to be sensitive to the fact that some people in the group may have higher standing than others. Sometimes you'll want to give those people the first chance to talk and other times you may want to allow everyone an equal opportunity to comment.

### PRIORITIZING RESPONSES

If you ask specific participants to speak first, you should do it in a way that doesn't show favoritism and also doesn't let others in the meeting feel like they have to mirror the initial response.

- I'll ask [name of person] to offer his comments first. [Name of person] has probably been involved in this issue more than anyone else in the group. We will hear from the rest of you next, and don't be afraid to offer a conflicting opinion. I'd rather hear a range of opinions to be sure we don't overlook some key considerations.
- We'll start our comments with the group leaders, as they have the most experience. But I'd like everyone to feel free to offer your opinion. Sometimes someone newer to the group sees things in a new light that opens up everyone's thinking.

### EQUAL INPUT TO ALL

You should try and allay any fears that more experienced people in the group might have that they are being overlooked or being taken for granted.

- I know some of you have more experience than others, but I think we will just go around clockwise and get everyone's input. Try to limit your comments to no more than three or four points so we have time to hear from everyone.
- I think that often the less experienced members of the group tend to have new ideas that challenge our somewhat ingrained ways of thinking, so let's start our comments with our newest employee.

## DRAWING OUT MORE INPUT

You want to be able to bring out more input for two reasons: first, to help people who might be intimidated by speaking, and second, because it is difficult to get buy-in from the group for later action if the members feel they weren't able to voice their views.

- Id like to hear at least one or two comments supporting your point of view.
- How will this affect your major objectives?
- Will this impact the program you started recently?
- Can you offer a little more background on your point?
- Do you see some specific benefits/problems in this situation?

# Controlling the Dominators

Most groups have at least a few difficult people who can disrupt a meeting. As a supervisor you can't just hope that these people don't cause too much trouble and you definitely can't cater to them. That only causes friction with the other members of the group. You need to confront problem people and handle the situation. Once you do, subsequent meetings will go more smoothly.

Four types of people try to dominate and consequently disrupt meetings: bullies, prima donnas, people who are passive-aggressive, and people who are overly negative.

## BULLIES

Bullies are often people who have been around a long time and been passed over for key positions. They can become hostile if challenged. In a one-on-one meeting, you can afford to let these people blow off a little steam, but not in a meeting with others, since those others may be negatively affected. You need to confront the bullies, deal with the situation, and set boundaries.

- We are all on even footing here and everyone needs to treat the others with respect.
- I'm not sure I'm hearing your point, [name of person]. I'm afraid I'm concentrating on how you are stating your point rather than on what you are saying. Do you want to take a breath and try again to explain your point?
- I don't think that this type of interaction with the group is going help us meet our goals here today.

## PRIMA DONNAS

People who act like prima donnas usually have experience and knowledge, but tend to keep facts and key contacts to themselves and want to be kept center stage. Sometimes prima donnas have special contacts and information that is important to your group. You need to offer them some praise, but not enough to encourage their sense of importance.

- We appreciate your insight, [name of person]. But we want to consider that with the input from the rest of our group. Things are in a state of transition and we have to be aware that some of our old-line contacts may not understand accurately how things will look in six months.
- Certainly, [name of person], your information has played a key role in the company's past decision making. But in today's world any strategy has a half life of only 18 to 24 months, so while keeping our old contacts we have to look forward to find where the next trend will be.

## PASSIVE-AGGRESSIVE PEOPLE

These people make small remarks to undermine your authority and take action that sabotages your efforts. They do this often in subtle, indirect ways that make it awkward to confront them directly; if you do, they will deny any questionable intent. The most common ways in which a passive-aggressive will act in meetings are to use body language that conflicts with what he or she is saying, to make sniping comments at others that undermine their position, or to fail to do his or her part and then offer excuses for failing.

A passive-aggressive type might say, "Well, you are the boss, I'll go along and do what you want," but then pout for the rest of the meeting. An example of a sniping comment might be "We'll have to start calling you the rising superstar—you seem to know so much more than anyone else." If a passive-aggressive person is given an assignment for the group that he or she doesn't like, a typical reaction might be to take on another task as a "favor" for another department or group and then tell you he or she didn't have time to do the assignment.

Passive-aggressive people hide their true reasoning and feelings behind a façade. You deal with such people by forcing out their true feelings and addressing them. Don't expect one meeting to turn around someone who is passive-aggressive; you can only make progress over a 6- to 12-month period.

- [Name of person], your body language tells me that what you just said isn't true. Tell me what you really think so we can deal with the issue. We won't get along if I can't trust what you are telling me.
- Was that remark sarcastic? I don't understand what you are trying to say. I have trouble effectively communicating with you when what I hear you saying and what you think you are saying are not the same.
- Let me tell you my impression when you tell me you took on added responsibilities without talking to me. I feel you didn't like your assignment or the project and you found a way to derail it. I could be wrong, but that's how I see it. I feel your actions are unacceptable for a member of this team.

## OVERLY NEGATIVE PEOPLE

These people are negative about contributions made by anyone else; the only ones they value are their own. They try to get their way by opposing in a calm manner (unlike the bully) and usually without any personal attacks. They often like to frame their negativity with justifying comments, such as "Let me play the devil's advocate for a moment."

- I appreciate your concerns. But at the moment we are looking for solutions to our challenges. None of those solutions will have all green lights telling us to move ahead. In fact most of the lights will be red. We need to concentrate on the positive aspects of each solution.

- The trouble with focusing on negative concerns is that it has a tendency to force us to stand still; and if we don't generate momentum, our group will become less and less effective. I, for one, hope our group can take on a leadership role. So let's look for ways to think outside the box and find new ways to succeed.

# Keeping Focused on Expectations

There are three expectations to keep in mind. The first is to keep to the schedule for the meeting, which should be included (with a start time and a stop time) on the agenda you distributed to the participants either in advance or at the beginning of the meeting. The second is for participants to conduct themselves appropriately during the meeting. The third is for the meeting to produce specific results.

## TIME EXPECTATIONS

Agenda items are worth only so much time and you don't want discussion to impede progress or dissension over a minor issue to disrupt your group. If it looks like the time spent on an item might exceed the time allocated, move to keep the meeting on schedule. Be prepared to do this early in the meeting if necessary.

- I've set two hours aside for the meeting as I don't want this topic to consume too much of our time. Let's try to confine our remarks to two to three minutes each. If you need to take more time, make your points succinctly.
- We all have a lot on our plate at this time, so we need to focus on finishing the meeting in the time allotted. We don't want to stray off the issue onto any tangents.

## MEETING BEHAVIOR EXPECTATIONS

In your opening comments, you should have communicated your expectations of appropriate behavior. Enforce those expectations: if any participants stray, focus them back on task.

- I really wanted everyone to have a chance to participate in this meeting. I'm hoping we can find a creative way to address this topic and I think some insights from people not as familiar with this issue might really help us see new ways to address this recurring problem.
- Thanks for your input. But as I stated at the beginning of the meeting, we are going to get everyone's comments first, then put those in categories, and then discuss those points. I don't want anyone interrupting people when they have the floor. You'll have your chance to comment once we start to discuss our potential action items.

## MEETING RESULTS EXPECTATIONS

You set goals for meetings. Unfortunately, often participants will start taking a meeting in another direction or go off on a tangent that they feel is relevant. If you want meetings to be productive, you have to keep the participants on course throughout the entire meeting.

- The goal for this meeting is to address this issue [specify the issue]. While your point might be valid, I don't think it is relevant to what we are trying to accomplish today. Unless you can tie the two topics together, I think we should just move back to today's issue.
- I'm starting to get confused by some of the discussion. This meeting was called to address this issue, [specify the issue]. I don't understand how these other issues relate to our topic. Perhaps you could each put together a short memo for distribution to the others in the group, and we can decide at a later meeting if those other issues are worth taking some additional action steps.

# Chapter 4
# Ensuring Group Support for Your Action Plan

B y now you are probably already thinking, "Wow, meetings are a lot of work!" Yes, meetings take a lot of work if you want good results. As a manager, you need to control the meeting, to keep the group on track so as to leave plenty of time to develop action plans and gather commitments from group members. You need for the participants to accept the action plan, accept their individual responsibilities, be willing to fulfill them, and support your goals.

This chapter deals with getting support and commitment. Participants will sometimes resist, an issue addressed in Chapter 5, "Dealing with Difficulties."

## Building Group Buy-in for an Action Plan

You will do much better at getting individual commitments if you can get the group to buy into your action plan. To get their buy-in, you must give the members a chance to comment on the action plan and feel that they at least were heard. In Chapter 2, in the section, "Setting the Stage for Action," I mentioned that you should always get possible solutions out on the table first, with minimal discussion. If you allow too much conversation during the presentation of ideas, the meeting will bog down. Once you have the ideas listed (and don't be afraid to list "do nothing" as an option), you are ready to discuss the ideas and determine which action plan to implement.

### WHEN THERE'S ONLY YOUR ACTION PLAN

In request-for-action meetings, you have a plan and you have actions detailed. You still need to give the group members a chance to discuss the plan, as they are more likely to buy into the plan if they feel you are open to input from them.

- Because of the time pressures, I have prepared this action plan and I firmly believe we need to move forward with it. But you have extensive experience and can provide different insights. I don't want to miss out on a chance to improve the plan. So I'll open up the floor to any suggestions any of you may have.

- Normally I would have had you work together to formulate our action plan. But in this case I'm trying to meet specific needs of our board and several other groups in the organization that have agendas many of you may not be aware of. Still, I'd like your input, and I'd like to have latitude to change our tasks and plans. I might not be able to accept a suggestion if it's at odds with other agendas in the organization. Try to be tolerant with me if that should happen.

## WHEN THERE ARE SEVERAL ACTION PLANS TO CONSIDER

In this situation, the interaction flows more freely and you can let discussion go on longer. I always like to focus on one idea first to try to save time. Focusing on group consensus also can preclude long discussions of plans that interest only one or two participants.

- Before starting to discuss the proposed action plans, I'd like each of you to take a half sheet of paper and indicate which plan you favor. If most, or all, of us are in favor of one plan, we might as well start discussing that plan first. We can still modify the action with tactics from the other action plans.
- We have a lot of good action items on the table. We should be able to create a strong plan from them. Let's start with the items that were listed by three or more of you and then decide what other actions we might want to add.

## ACTIONS WITH MODIFICATIONS FROM DISCUSSION

If you want buy-in, it is always wise to adjust your initial plan at least a little. You don't need to get every participant to agree with the final result, but you want them all to feel they had a chance to offer input.

- I believe this plan is a step up from our starting point and I appreciate all the input. I know we don't all agree on every point, but I think we considered all points of view. Does everyone agree that the plan as outlined captures the essence of our discussion?
- I'm pleased with the way we worked through these issues and I feel confident about our action for moving forward. If you all agree, we will move on to individual commitments.

## Soliciting Individual Commitments

Without a commitment to actions and tasks from individuals, meetings are often a waste of time. Once you decide on some action from a meeting, you need a commitment from each person assigned a task that he or she will complete that task.

### MAKING A REQUEST FOR COMMITMENT

Meeting participants often seem surprised if they are asked to commit to taking action. Your request can come across as bossy to some people, so you might want to make a statement that will make your request more acceptable.

- I don't believe you can expect action from anyone unless that person specifically commits to meeting that expectation. Let's just go around the room and each of you can state the specific action you are committing to complete.

- Just to clarify my notes and to be sure we are all on the same page, I'd appreciate if you each send me an e-mail with your action commitments from this meeting. I may get back to you if your commitment doesn't match what I'm expecting from you.

### INCREASING THE EXTENT OF THE COMMITMENT

You may not always need this, but often meeting participants will express a commitment to action that is less than you expect or less than you feel the person is capable of doing.

- I was really hoping you would commit to more than that. I'm not sure your commitment is enough to really meet the project's goals. Are there some other projects you can delay or that we can pass on to others so you can increase your commitment?

■ Is there any way you can raise the level of action you are promising? I was counting on you to [state your expectation]. What do you need from me or others in the group to meet that commitment?

## ASKING FOR ADDITIONAL HELP

You should be on a roll, with group members committing to actions and looking very much like they're taking charge. Now is a good time to ask if anyone without a commitment will agree to helping one of the others, or possibly taking an additional action you hadn't expected.

■ Now that all our commitments are out on the table, I think we can see that there is much to do. Can any of you offer to do something additional to support the overall project or help others execute their tasks?

■ It sounds like we have strong commitments for action. Can anyone, especially those of you without a commitment, do anything more for the project? If any of you have ideas that will facilitate the project, now is the time to speak up.

## Confirming the Action Plan Schedule

Everything seems in order up to this point: you have an action plan, commitments, and group buy-in. Your last step is to confirm that all members of the group agree to a schedule. You should keep a running record of the action plan or ask someone when the meeting starts to record the action plan as it develops and then to read it back to the group near the end of the meeting.

### CHECKING FOR MISSING ITEMS

The first step is to make sure your action plan is not missing any items.

- I'll be sending out a detailed action schedule after the meeting, but I want to read what we have down first just to be sure we haven't left anything off the list. Let me know if I've left off an action item we've discussed or if you think of any other items that we have forgotten.

- [Name of person] has been keeping our action list as we've been talking. [Name of person], can you read the list over now? As the rest of you listen, make sure the action plan is right for your tasks and that nothing is missing from your assignment.

### CHECKING FOR CONFLICTS

As your action plan becomes more complex, the chances of conflicts increase. You don't want people later on to use conflicts in the schedule as an excuse for not completing their assignments.

- I just want to do a quick check here. Does anyone see any conflicts within this schedule or with anything you have scheduled to do? If so, let's deal with it now.
- This action plan needs to be a high priority for all of us. Does anyone see any conflicts that could jeopardize their chances of keeping to the schedule? After the meeting, I'd also like each of you to review your schedule and action dates and get back to me immediately if you have a conflict.

## CHECKING FOR TIMING ISSUES

The last thing to check is timing: can everyone complete his or her task on time? You want action results, so you must pin down commitments to action and the schedule so you can count on tasks being done on time.

- A final consideration is timing. Does anyone have a timing issue with the plan, an action date you can't meet? This is a chance to bring up and resolve any problem. Otherwise, I'll expect that all of you will meet all of the dates listed.
- Our group and other groups in the organization are going to count on this plan being executed on schedule. Does anyone have an issue with the timing that we should discuss?

# Chapter 5
# Dealing with Difficulties

Many of the perfect phrases in the first four chapters are intended to ease fears, overcome resistance, and spur people to action they may be reluctant to take. People tend to want to stay in their comfort zones and are not always interested in moving in a new direction.

This chapter is about severe resistance and reactions that can be disruptive and make a meeting less effective, or even a disaster. You must be prepared to handle these difficulties in a professional manner that keeps the meetings moving and the tone positive.

# Working with Participants Opposed to the Action Plan

Frequently, people are opposed to an action plan or prefer another plan. They will generally go along with the group consensus or your decision, but sometimes they will continue to voice strong opposition.

As supervisor you have the option of simply telling those opposed that the group will implement the plan, period. But that approach doesn't help you build group camaraderie.

I recommend you first ensure that all members of the group share the same goals, then ask for alternative suggestions to achieve your goals, and finally—as a last resort—explain that group consensus is not necessary to move ahead.

## GOVERNING GOALS OR PRIORITIES

Often, disputes over action are because people don't share the same goal. If you can clarify the group's goals, you can frequently reduce or eliminate resistance. These goals and priorities can be set by you, the group, or someone outside the group, such as top management or an outside stakeholder.

For example, if you have a meeting regarding marketing budgets and priorities, to determine where to allocate money in the next year, disagreement is likely as all parties will want more money for their projects. The goals for the group or organization might be prioritized as follows:

- 10% sales growth
- 2% increase in margins
- Increase market share in a developing application

If someone objects that his or her project is not receiving enough money, you can reiterate that the money must be focused on projects that grow sales, increase margins, or increase market share in a target application.

- I understand that you don't agree with our plan. And I understand that our decisions will have a negative effect on some of your goals, but we have to work toward our priorities and goals. We need to [specify goal or priority]. I'm willing to listen if you can demonstrate how we can better hit that target.

- You have given some reasons for opposing this action. I'm tied up in trying to meet our number-one priority: [specify item]. Can you do me a favor and recast your arguments so they relate to hitting our priorities? Those are the arguments that might sway the group to your point of view.

## SOLICITING ALTERNATIVE SUGGESTIONS

A second choice is to ask people who disagree with the action plan to suggest another action plan. Then you can rate the plans by how well they meet the group's priorities. Always try to judge the recommendations against something concrete—priorities or objectives are best—to ensure that your decision is unbiased.

- Do you have an alternative suggestion? I'm happy to consider other plans you might want to recommend. But before you put in your recommendation, be sure to think about which priority it represents or serves. We won't move forward with actions that target the wrong priority.

- No plan has all green lights and, as you have pointed out, our plans have some red lights. I'm willing to hear other suggestions for moving forward. But eliminating negatives isn't enough; we also need to be sure the plan shows strong potential for meeting our goals.

## ESTABLISHING THAT CONSENSUS IS NOT REQUIRED

In the end, it's not necessary that every participant agree with the result of a meeting, and often there will be people who don't agree. To move forward, you don't need to achieve unanimous support of the result; you just need to ensure that most participants support it.

- We don't need to have you all agree to move ahead. The only point I was firm on coming into the meeting was our priority for what we had to accomplish. I was open to any suggestions that would help us achieve that goal. I feel that you have all had a chance to have your say. Now it is time to move on.

- For me consensus just means that most members of the group agree. I know there is some opposition, but I think it is clear that most of us support this action plan and it is now time for all of us to get behind the decision and support it.

## Overcoming a Lack of Commitment

Far more difficult to handle than opposition is lack of commitment. It may be due to disinterest. It may also be because people are afraid of standing out or making a mistake. Sometimes people don't know what to do and so they do not agree to do anything.

Getting commitment from people who are disinterested, afraid, or confused is difficult but not impossible. The best course of action is to remove the safety of inaction, reward those who commit, and offer help without causing anybody embarrassment.

### REMOVING THE SAFETY OF INACTION

Many people have learned that the safest course of action is to not commit to any, since taking action means taking a risk of getting blamed. You need to put people on notice at meetings that doing nothing is not a safe option.

- Just as a point of reference, our group and I get judged by how we respond to situations that call for immediate action. This is also part of my review process. Certainly we all have times when we can't act, but that should be the exception rather than the rule.

- The commitments made so far are not going to get us where we need to go. What worries me is that some of you have responsibilities that periodically call on you to go above and beyond what you normally do. Based on what I see today, I may need to realign responsibilities so I'm not being left high and dry. All of you, please take a moment to consider what tasks you could let slip to make the commitments we need today.

## REWARDING PARTICIPANTS WHO COMMIT

Rewards don't have to be big; I've found that just taking the big contributors out to lunch is reward enough. You simply want participants who are slow to commit to fear being left out and to become more receptive to getting involved.

- OK, I guess the three of you (indicate or name three persons) are the "go squad" with me on this project. We don't have all the assignments worked out, but let's go out to lunch tomorrow and figure out a way to get the jobs done. I still would like one more person to help out with [specify item]. Last chance for a volunteer!

- I appreciate you stepping forward to tackle the project. That is the type of can-do spirit that makes someone a strong management candidate (or "strong manager" if more appropriate). We still have some work to do to make sure all the bases are covered, but let's meet in my office tomorrow to talk about. There's no point holding up the others in the group who are not going to get involved.

## OFFERING HELP TACTFULLY

There are times when you need someone to do something, but he or she has a problem with it. Rather than risk a big disagreement in front of the others in the group, state instead that you will meet with the person in the next few days to help complete his or her assignment. While you may be only postponing an eventual disagreement, any disagreement will be one on one so neither you nor the worker will lose face with the others.

- Before you give an adamant no, I believe I have some help that will enable you to take on the tasks. I'll check my schedule and e-mail you to arrange a time that we can meet tomorrow.

- I can't promise for sure, but I think I might be able to get someone in another group to help you. Let me check tonight and let's meet tomorrow and see if that person is available. If I can't arrange to get someone to help, I'll figure out how to free some of my time to help you finish your tasks.

# Handling Difficult People

The Chapter 3 section, "Controlling the Dominators," addressed dealing with difficult people by controlling them during discussions. This section deals with handling difficult people when finalizing responsibilities, actions, or some other function of the group.

Once again the four personality types that can disrupt the end of a meeting are bullies, prima donnas, passive-aggressive types, and people who are overly negative.

## BULLIES

People who bully are usually not team players and are often negative. Typically they will either try to take over a project, becoming in effect the team leader, or try to degrade others who are signing up for a project. If you allow the bully to take charge, nobody else will want to be on the team. Bullies who want to take over might say something like "Look, I've worked on five projects just like this and every time we got the job done. I don't think [name of person] has the right experience and he is going to make some big mistakes."

■ Thanks, [name of person]. I appreciate your willingness to take on the whole project. But there is a lot of work to do here, so I would prefer to have a team do this assignment. Let me keep your offer in mind, see what the others can do, and then come back and see what tasks make sense for you.

■ (If someone makes a disparaging remark). [Name of person], I really appreciate that [name of person disparaged] is willing to pitch in and help the group. I'm pretty sure he/she can do the assignment but if troubles arise, he/she can get help from me or other members of the group.

## PRIMA DONNAS

They want to be the center of attention, dominating the end result of the meeting, trying to take charge of the entire action. With a prima donna, respond very much as you would to a bully. Comments relating to your goals and priorities, as discussed earlier in the section on overcoming resistance to the plan, can often put an end to any attempts to refocus the meeting.

If someone tries to refocus action on his or her agenda:

- [Name of person], I think we covered earlier that we need to stay with the action we have identified that meets our priorities. I don't think it's worthwhile going backwards; instead, we need to keep going forward. Is that OK with you?
- Thanks, [name of person]. I appreciate your expertise and what you have to offer in leading the project. I feel this is an area where things are changing rapidly and we need the input of many people, so I really think the project is better served if we take a team approach.

## PASSIVE-AGGRESSIVE PEOPLE

The indirect comments of people acting passive-aggressively thinly disguise what they are really saying and can drive anyone to distraction, especially if their comments cause confusion. The best way to deal with this behavior is to confront the person about what he or she means.

- [Name of person], I'm confused. Where do you stand on this issue? You've told me that you support this action, but I'm picking up signals from your tone and body language that you don't.
- Let's try to keep our comments related to keeping the meeting and project going forward. I don't have the patience to start over. We've decided on what we want to do; now we need to decide who will do what. I'd appreciate it if we keep the meeting on task.

## OVERLY NEGATIVE PEOPLE

People will be negative, stating that their efforts will not work or that the project as planned will fail. Usually they won't propose any alternative solutions. The best way to minimize negative remarks is by letting such people see how their negative reactions do not help the organization.

- If our only solution is to do nothing, I have to ask why we are getting paid (or why people have entrusted us with responsibilities). Anyone can just continue to say nothing will work.
- I can't see how you can create anything positive when you approach the situation in such a negative manner. I have to believe that someone with less experience and expertise, but a positive attitude, will have a much better chance of success. If you must persist in this, at least try to find one or two reasons why something might work before you shoot it down.

## Part Two

# Managing Meetings with Peers and Supervisors

For most people, managing meetings with peers and supervisors presents both tremendous risk and reward. Without great care, you can lose control of the meeting and look very ineffective, harming your image and your career. In my mind there is no doubt that if you can run a productive meeting and keep things under control, you will look like a rising star. You will show the confidence, management and people skills, and overall organizational control that will label you as a future leader.

# Chapter 6
# Opening Remarks

When you are running a meeting with peers and supervisors or other superiors, you need to take control immediately. Typically at least a few peers and perhaps superiors with their own agenda will try to dominate the meeting. Others will try to push you through your agenda before you can explain what you are trying to accomplish.

When you are in charge of any type of meetings, be sure to thank everyone for coming and introduce anyone others may not know. Also have the participants introduce themselves if there are many who don't know each other or if you have a superior attending who may not know all of your peers.

## Setting the Tone

The opening minutes of a meeting are crucial to establishing control. You need this segment to be brief, optimally less than one minute, in case a superior arrives late, which means you may have to repeat the opening one time and sometimes more than one time. Concentrate on four points: an opening comment to establish why you are holding the meeting, a softening statement that shows you are not over-stepping your authority, an explanation of the structure of the meeting, and finally a comment soliciting buy-in to your approach.

### OPENING COMMENT

You want to establish your authority to run the meeting, but in a way that does not alienate your peers or overstep your responsibility. Typically the best way to do that is to name the source of your authority to call the meeting. This could be a superior, another group in the organization, a customer, a user of your services, or another type of stakeholder. You may also have called the meeting yourself at the suggestion of a superior.

- I received a request from [customer, stakeholder, superior, or other department] to[state purpose of meeting] …
- I was asked by [name of person] to [action] …
- [Name of person] approached me to find a solution to [state problem] …
- I brought a situation regarding [issue] to the attention of [superior or other stakeholder], who suggested that I call together the meeting today to [state purpose] …

## SOFTENING STATEMENT

When you are running a meeting and you are not the boss, it is likely some of your peers will feel you are taking on too much authority and your supervisors will want to be sure you are not overstepping your bounds. You should act as a facilitator rather than as a boss. It is best to do this as the finishing phrase to your opening comment, so each of these phrases finishes off the corresponding opening comment above.

- … to bring the customers' need for [state specific need] to the attention of key people so the organization can respond.

- … to help coordinate efforts in a department to respond to [state situation].

- … to work with people throughout the company to find a way to [state specific objective].

- … to facilitate communications among departments in order to expedite the project.

## FOLLOWING AN AGENDA

You have an objective for your meeting and you need to keep control to attain that objective. The easiest way to do that is to follow an agenda and limit the remarks until after your presentation. The statements listed here concentrate on the need to follow an agenda.

- I know you are all busy and I think the best way for us to cover the agenda and get out in a reasonable time is to start with a short presentation and then give everyone a chance for comment.

- I have prepared a short presentation that will highlight key information that I hope will help us in our decision process. If you hold your comments until after the presentation, we can avoid discussing a point that will be covered later in the presentation.
- The results of this meeting are important to [customer, stakeholder, superior, or other department]. In order to have enough time to discuss the action plan we will propose, I suggest we hold comments until after my short presentation.

## SOLICITING BUY-IN

You've just started the meeting and the participants probably are still in a cooperative mood. So finish the opening by asking them to agree to your request to hold comments now. It will help you keep control of the early phases of the meeting and it will help ease your peers' fears you are taking on too much authority.

- Does this format work for everyone?
- If nobody objects to holding all comments until after the presentation, I'll proceed. (Wait five to ten seconds for comments.)
- If we can hold comments, I believe the presentation can answer most of your questions. Does everyone agree?

## Stating Overall Goals

State your overall goals in general terms. For example, the goal of the meeting is "to see if we can find a way to help our third-largest customer" or "I hope that the information I present will allow you to prepare your sales and marketing plans." Since your overall goals vary by meeting, I've listed phrases based upon the five meeting types I use throughout the book.

- Informational
- Team building
- Problem solving
- Request for action
- Task review

### INFORMATIONAL

Generally, informational meetings are meant to bring participants up to speed about something that could impact your organization.

- The goal of the meeting is to first share some new information.
- I'd like to start out by sharing some results.
- Let's start by going over some indications that our situation is changing.

### TEAM BUILDING

These meetings are usually with people who don't work well together and are difficult to manage. Use the term "team building" very sparingly; instead, concentrate on a task ahead for which the team members will need to cooperate.

- I've been asked to see if we can improve our communication and cooperation within the team so we will be in a better position to cope with the upcoming changes in [specify situation].

- I believe we all feel the pressure of having too many things to do, while at the same time we have new challenges coming. I had a specific request from [name of person] to see if the team can figure out ways we can cooperate more effectively to improve the situation.

- [Name of person who put you in charge of meeting] feels our group is not presenting a united front to other departments and feels this has hurt everyone's productivity.

## PROBLEM SOLVING

This is the type of meeting that is easiest to call and lead, as taking quick action can often avoid or resolve small issues before they become major problems.

- A situation has come up that currently is a small issue, but I thought our group might want to address it before it becomes a problem.

- I have had several problems lately with [describe situation] that concerned me. Then I heard two others mention the same problem, so I thought maybe we could address this situation within our group.

- I'm having a major problem that is affecting my performance and I'm hoping that you might be able to help me find a solution.

## REQUEST FOR ACTION

This is one of the more common situations where you might lead a meeting with peers and superiors, requesting support and action to address an area under your responsibility.

- Right now I'm in charge of the new product release [be specific] and I am going to need each of you to support me with specific actions to meet the goals I've been given.

- I was asked by [name of stakeholder] to monitor a situation [be specific] and alert him/her to developments. Before doing that, I thought we should meet and discuss what action we should take.

- On [specify date] the organization is going to face [be specific]. I believe we all want to see our group play a leadership role and I was hoping we could create an action plan for that role.

## TASK REVIEW

In these meetings, also called progress updates, focus your efforts on achieving your overall goal on an action approved previously or a request for action from a superior or other stakeholder.

- I just wanted a short meeting so we can update each other on how we are proceeding with our efforts for [name the superior, other department, stakeholder, or customer] regarding [specify project].

- It has been about [state time] since we last gave an update to [be specific] on the [name of project]. I'd like to show that we are making progress.

- I've heard some comments from [name of person] wondering whether or not this project was ever going to get off the ground. I just wanted to get an update from everyone here to see what response I can offer.

## Specifying Expectations

You've mentioned an overall goal to provide a little background. Now you need to immediately specify what you expect from the meeting. For example, "The customer has requested that we come back to him with an action plan by May 1. To do that, at this meeting we need to determine the action plan that we will propose."

### INFORMATIONAL

You don't want to have a meeting to share information that you could have sent out in an e-mail. So you want to have some commitment for future action.

- I've asked you to come together today because I felt this new information might help us find two or three tactics today that could help improve our performance.

- From my conversations with others over the last week, I've found people are spinning this data in radically different ways. I'm hoping we can discuss the data and then see if we can create a unified statement about how this data affects us.

### TEAM BUILDING

Peers can be effective in a team-building meeting only by attacking a specific target, an effort that requires better teamwork. Team building also works best when you can focus on common goals.

- I hope that at the end of the meeting we can develop a joint front that will give our group's needs and goals a higher priority in the coming reorganization.

- I know I feel like you do, so overburdened that I could easily slip into a negative pattern. Hopefully, we can all see that we are in the same boat and can find a way to make sure we are all pulling in the same direction.

## PROBLEM SOLVING

You must react to problems with specific actions from each member that can potentially solve the problem. Each member must buy into his or her role in the plan if you expect to get positive results.

- Hopefully we can walk out of this meeting with an action plan that we can all agree will solve the problem, with a commitment from each of us regarding our individual roles and responsibilities.

- I don't have a solution to the problem in mind, but I'm hoping we can put our heads together and come up with a plan today. Any delay on our part is bound to bring complaints from [customer, stakeholder, superior, or other department].

- I know this problem is my responsibility, but I can't seem to resolve it on my own. I hope all of you in this room can work with me to generate specific actions that you and I can take to address the problem.

## REQUEST FOR ACTION

Your agenda should detail your expectations. Everyone will understand the objective when a meeting is titled, for example, "Preparing for the May 20 Launch of [specify action item]." What is important in request-for-action meetings is getting a commitment from each participant to finish his or her task on time.

- Since our goal is clear, I hope to leave the meeting with key interim target dates that we must meet in order for the project to succeed. I need each of you to indicate when you will finish your tasks.

- We will need to complete an implementation chart by the end of the meeting that all of us here will buy into and agree to meet.

- We have no choice but to meet our deadline. I realize our time is much shorter than we are all used to working with. I know the schedule we create today will ask all groups to compromise and truncate their schedules. I know it will be difficult, but I will appreciate your cooperation and support.

## TASK REVIEW

The final expectation of a task review is almost always to readjust, based upon what has happened since the last meeting, to achieve whatever objectives have been set by you, your superior, or the group.

- I'd like to finalize my report about our progress on this task [be specific] and where and why we have fallen behind, and then include with the report an implementation plan that will put us back on schedule.

- [Name of person or group] feels affected by our apparent lack of progress. At the end of the meeting, I'd like to be able to send a status update, including where we are now according to our original schedule, our projected completion date, any new action items we are proposing, and an explanation for any delays.

# Chapter 7
# The Presentation

Most likely, you will make a presentation. But the meeting may also include presentations by others. These presentations may not be supportive of your view; it is possible they may even conflict with your presentation. So right out of the box you may face some problems in running the meeting smoothly.

I recommend that you prepare one or two sheets of attachments to the agenda with graphs or bulleted points that compellingly state the case for your take on the situation to be discussed at the meeting. For example, if a customer has complained that your company has missed its delivery schedule, make a chart that compares the organization's delivery performance this year versus last and then make a bulleted list of dates of customer complaints. You can refer back to those attachments if others try to take you off task, so you can keep the meeting following your agenda.

## Reinforcing Your Take

If you expect opposition in a meeting, you should strengthen your position by mentioning a supportive view from an important stakeholder whose opinion the group will value. If you don't have a view from an important stakeholder before the meeting, try to meet with one, show your presentation, and get his or her input. You'll do much better at the meeting if you can say, "I met with [name of person] yesterday and he/she felt that it appeared our performance regarding [area] has slipped since last year."

### INFORMATIONAL

Explain why a stakeholder wanted you to present the information or how a stakeholder reacted when you gave him or her a pre-meeting presentation.

- [Stakeholder] and top management have been pleased with our performance the first half of the year. I reviewed this presentation early this week with [stakeholder] and he feels that it pinpoints some of the specific areas where we've excelled.

- Before presenting this information, I reviewed it with [stakeholder] to be sure I had captured the information she wanted me to present. She was somewhat alarmed that the situation regarding [area] shows we are even further off course than she thought.

### TEAM BUILDING

If you are in charge of team building with peers or supervisors, it's probably because you have run other team-building meetings or have experience with this particular team-building exercise. Since there are always a few people who resist team building, you should emphasize your experience. I've also found it helpful to call up references provided by the vendors of the team-building exercise or talk with the writer of the article or book where you found the team-building exercise, to get some positive quotes to start the presentation.

- I've called up some of the references for the team-building program to see how it worked for them. [Contact] of [organization] told me 80 percent of their employees surveyed after the exercise gave it a positive rating.

- [Stakeholder one] and [stakeholder two] had a chance to use this program at [location]. They felt the program provided key insights into some of the factors that disrupt group communications and they highly recommended we use this program.

## PROBLEM SOLVING

Your agenda and attachments will let people know the problem that you're addressing and indicate how serious it is. What you want to do now is mention how quickly the problem needs to be resolved and whether you believe that the problem should be addressed by a small group or task force or if all or most members of the group need to be involved.

- [Customer], our major customer, has been complaining about this situation to us for three months and has demanded a solution within the next six weeks. I worry that our group won't be able to respond in time, and I think that everyone here must make it a priority to meet this deadline.

- [Stakeholder] wants a solution on the table before the start of the next quarter. The issue is complex and, after talking with [your supervisor or other stakeholder], I don't believe we can resolve the issue with a large group. We will need a special task force to deal with it.

## REQUEST FOR ACTION

You best approach is to first state that you have a goal to meet and that you can't meet that goal without help from the group. That's the take you are communicating.

■ I've been charged with the responsibility of [be specific]. Right now I'm not going to be able to take hold of the situation on my own. My presentation highlights the situation and some of the help I feel I could use to achieve my goal. But I'm open to any suggestions or even another approach.

■ I've asked you to meet because I need help. A problem we have is [be specific]. I don't have a solution, but the problem definitely needs to be addressed. I'll do a short presentation to bring you up to speed on the problem. Then I'll open the floor up to your suggestions and alternative actions.

## TASK REVIEW

You could be in charge of a task review because you have an important task or you could be in charge because the responsibility for leading the meeting rotates. Your take on the meeting should be that it is either a task review for the completion of a task or just a general review.

■ My main interest in this meeting is to see that all of the tasks supporting this project are on schedule so that I can be sure to meet my deadlines. I'd appreciate it if, after your presentation, each of you could mention any problem areas. Hopefully, we will be able to put together a chart of problem areas and proposed corrective actions that can be tracked until our next meeting.

- For your presentations, we will be going in alphabetical order. Feel free to make any comments or ask questions at the end of the presentation. At the end of the discussion, we can all decide whether or not we need to propose any specific actions.

## Preparing Participants for the Presentation

For obvious reasons, the meeting participants often won't be as receptive to a peer or a subordinate as they would to a superior, so you need to preface your presentation so they know better what is at stake and what will be expected from them. If you don't do this in advance, the resulting discussion may be less focused and productive.

### INFORMATIONAL

You should try to engage the group in some specific actions after the presentation or later in the meeting. Otherwise, participants may lose interest.

■ [Stakeholder] has asked me to check with the group to see if anyone feels this information indicates any potential roadblocks for the West Coast region's expansion plans. We will discuss that issue at the end of the meeting.

■ I don't believe we need any action at this meeting, but [stakeholder] wanted to be sure you include any key facts from this presentation in your reports and presentations for the annual meeting.

### TEAM BUILDING

In this type of meeting, usually you have interaction throughout the exercise and then a follow-up session. Your big worry is that some participants will not get involved in the exercise and ruin the experience for the others. The best way to motivate people is to explain the importance of involvement and to mention that you will be writing an analysis of the exercise after the meeting.

- This exercise won't work unless everyone participates throughout. If you stick with it all the way through, I believe we can all get a lot out of it. I have to report to [stakeholder] on our experience with this exercise and you will all get a chance to offer comments about it at the end.
- [Stakeholder] has received reports that this program has worked especially well at two other companies where he is on the board of directors. He has asked me for a report so he can compare our reactions and results.

## PROBLEM SOLVING

You want the group to address a problem reported by others. Start by saying where you acquired the data and then explain what type of problem solving you expect after the presentation.

- This information is based on interviews with three East Coast customers that have dropped their purchases from us by more than 50 percent. Once we get through analyzing their comments, and the products they are buying in place of our products, I think we can do some brainstorming and then pick two or three choices as the starting point for an action plan.
- I've pulled together statistics from the quality control groups at our plants and compared their reports with the increase in quality complaints we are getting from our customer service and sales departments. The trends from the two groups don't match. [Stakeholder] has asked our group to figure out how to capture, with our plant quality checks, the quality problems now arising in the field.

## REQUEST FOR ACTION

You have already stated that you are looking for help. So you need to state that after your short presentation you'd welcome a free-flowing session in which participants propose and discuss specific action plans.

- I've tried to keep my presentation short, just to give you a feel for the issues involved. After the presentation, please feel free to ask any questions about where we are right now. Then I'm hoping we will have an idea session to come up with potential action plans. I'm eager to hear everyone's ideas.

- I'll quickly review my situation. Then I'd appreciate any specific offers of help. After that, if you don't feel confident that we have a solution, perhaps we can conduct a short brainstorming session.

## TASK REVIEW

These meetings are held to ensure that action plans are working and projects are on schedule. If you have a series of reviews for a project, you want to allow short questions at the end of each review, but hold extended discussion for the end.

- Our goal today is to check on the overall progress for project [specify]. We have scheduled several task reviews. Ask any questions for clarification immediately after each presentation, but let's hold off on discussion until after all the presentations. If there are areas we feel may need help, we may be able to address them at the end of the meeting. If not, we may need to schedule a follow-up meeting.

- Most of us are involved with this project. As you listen to the review, please ensure that the completion dates will allow you to keep to your schedule. If not, let's discuss them at the end of the meeting so we can keep to our overall schedule.

## Preparing for Interaction

After the presentations, you will want to help prepare the group for taking some sort of action, both in the meeting and afterwards.

### ESTABLISHING THE AGENDA

Before discussion begins, you need to announce what will happen next. If possible, reiterate that your stakeholder requested the meeting.

- Before opening the floor for discussion, I'd like to briefly cover what we will try to accomplish next during the meeting, and then more specifically what [stakeholder] is counting on us to do after the meeting.

- [Stakeholder] provided the impetus for this meeting with his/her request that [specify]. We will discuss our formal response to [stakeholder], but let's try to keep our comments focused on his/her specific requests and not worry about assigning blame.

### DEALING WITH AN UNCOOPERATIVE GROUP

You can avoid or minimize negative reactions and encourage cooperation if you rely on the importance of the stakeholder who called for the meeting and if you announce that you will be writing up a report, so the participants know that any lack of cooperation may be noted.

- As I mentioned earlier, this meeting was occasioned by a request from [stakeholder], and I feel I need to report on the meeting. So I'd like to focus here on specific comments about how your activities may be contributing to the situation that has alarmed [stakeholder] and any actions you might propose to help turn the situation around.

■ I've been asked to compile an action report on the meeting for [stakeholder] . To simplify our discussions, I've prepared a chart I'll fill out that indicates what actions each of us might be able to take, and then I'll write a final summary to indicate that we have addressed the situation.

# Chapter 8
# Group Reaction and Participation

Typically, you can keep fairly good control of a meeting through the presentation, but you run the risk of the meeting slipping out of control once you invite interaction. If you try to take an authoritative tone, you may generate hostility among your peers and any supervisors, but if you do nothing to keep order, a discussion can easily go astray, become chaotic, and fail to lead to achieving your goals. You can maintain control if you can lead with people who support you, learn how to keep dominators in check without alienating them, and keep the meeting focused on your expectations.

## Targeting Supporters

Your best situation at a meeting is to have a supportive and protective supervisor present to keep the meeting moving toward your goals. If there's no supportive supervisor there, you may still be able to rely on peers who support your position. Starting the discussion on a positive note will often help the meeting continue smoothly.

### STARTING WITH SUPPORT FROM A SUPERVISOR

If a supervisor is going to attend the meeting, you should always go over your presentation with him or her prior to the meeting and cover any concerns at that time. Rely on the supervisor first to support your project.

- We need to next identify how we can use this information to improve our general stakeholder meeting. Let me ask [supervisor] first for his/her comments regarding the importance of this task and the results he/she would like from the meeting.

- I've had a chance to preview my presentation for [supervisor]. [Supervisor], do you have any comments to make before we start our discussion?

### WORKING WITH SUPPORTIVE PARTICIPANTS

If you know some of the participants are supportive, invite them to respond first after your presentation.

- [Participant], you've been tracking this project for a while and are familiar with many of the issues involved. Why don't you start the discussion with your view of the problem and suggestions for actions we can take?

## Group Reaction and Participation

■ I know most of you will have some comments about the cause of the problem, but I believe the real issue here is how we move forward. Let's start the comments with [participant] and then move around the room. After you've all had a chance to comment, we can start to plan what we should do next.

## Gathering Opinions from Everyone

One goal for any meeting should be that the participants, even those who disagree, feel the topic was discussed fairly and any decisions made were based on sound reasons. As a result, they will support the actions or responses determined at the meeting. Participants feel that way only if they believe their views were heard and considered. You need to be sensitive that some participants, for whatever reasons, feel that their input on a certain topic is especially valuable. You want them to feel you understand and appreciate the importance of their contributions.

### PRIORITIZING RESPONSES

Some people will try to dominate the meeting. One way to control their input somewhat is to ask for input from the group member with the most experience or responsibility in the topic area. You can also often elicit a more positive response if you treat his or her input as more important. If you plan on prioritizing someone's response, it is a good idea to meet with him or her before the meeting for input that you can include in your presentation.

- [Participant], this is a topic area in which you have the most experience with customers. Perhaps you'd like to share your ideas first on what you feel might be a creative solution.

- We had several other projects over the last few years covering similar situations. [Participant], you headed up some of those projects. Would you like to comment first on our proposal and offer any suggestions?

## ENSURING EQUAL OPPORTUNITY FOR INPUT

No meeting really ensures equal opportunity for all to provide input, but you can solicit ideas from all participants first before starting a discussion.

- What I'd like to do is go around the room and get a short overview response from each of you, maybe three or four sentences, so we can get an idea of what we all think about the proposal. Then we can discuss the proposal and our reactions to it.

- We have people here from several groups and I'm sure there are different points of view. Before opening up the floor to any detailed comments or proposals, let's get a one-minute snapshot from each of you so we all understand all the perspectives here.

## DRAWING OUT MORE INPUT

You have a goal for the meeting—an action plan, a request for support, or some other intended result. Maybe the participants have not offered enough suggestions or the discussion might have been disappointing. At this point you might want to propose an action plan, even (or especially) if you know that at least some participants will object to it, or you might want to ask specific questions.

- Since you all don't seem to feel strongly about how we proceed, I'd like to make a suggestion and then, if you all agree, I'll put that into our meeting notes.

- For my report I would like to include specific responses to the four questions that are the basis for this meeting. Let me just ask each question and then you can decide how we as a group will respond.

## Controlling the Dominators

To control a meeting, you need to beware of bullies, prima donnas, passive-aggressive people, and overly negative people. Your options for controlling peers and managers are few, but you definitely don't want to allow any participants to dominate the meeting, as that will only make the situation worse. You need to hold your own.

Often dominators, other than prima donnas, are like critics: they attack without assuming any responsibility. Dominators will often shrink to the sidelines if you can put the onus of action on them. Otherwise, you need to do all you can to neutralize them. (See Chapter 3 for descriptions of these four personalities.)

### BULLIES

If your supervisor or other superior attends the meeting, he or she may address the situation. Otherwise, you need to set and maintain boundaries.

- We have a lot to accomplish and I want to hold the meeting to our scheduled 90 minutes. I'm not sure this tone of discussion will get us anywhere.
- What I am hearing is your hostility, so I assume you are reacting negatively. What do you propose instead? I for one am open to your suggestions and I appreciate constructive feedback.

### PRIMA DONNAS

Prima donnas like to be at the center of the action and they will be more than happy to offer you a solution that puts them there. Prima donnas are typically intelligent and they sometimes offer effective comments and solutions, but you need to keep them from taking over. The key is to take the tack that the prima donnas have other responsibilities that are more important. If possible, get some support from your supervisor to strengthen your position.

- Thanks for that input and I appreciate your trying to take a leadership role here. But when this issue came up, I talked with [name of person] your [supervisor, preferably, or other stakeholder] and he/she felt I should take a lead because I could push some of my other responsibilities to the background. I'm sure he/she felt your projects were too important to delay.

- I know you've worked on projects like this before. Before the meeting, I requested the notes from meetings on those projects from your [supervisor or other person] and I found some things of interest. I'd like to discuss some points with you in the next week or two. But now I'd like to understand the views of others for whom I don't have any records to guide me.

## PASSIVE-AGGRESSIVE PEOPLE

These people are very tough to handle for someone who isn't a manager. You deal with them by moving them from the periphery to center stage or by always asking them clarifying or direct questions about their position.

- I take it from your tone that you are opposed to what we are discussing. Do you have an alternative view that you would like to offer? I'm open to a new approach.

**Note:** Passive-aggressive people will often say they are not opposed. If so, ask them what they like about what you've discussed and what they don't like. Either their opposition will come out or they will be boxed into support.

- I don't understand what you are trying to say. What specific actions or comments do you support and which do you not support?

**Note:** Passive-aggressive people will always deny that a comment was sarcastic.

## OVERLY NEGATIVE PEOPLE

Move these people away from attacking from the sidelines and into the center to propose solutions. They do not like to present their own ideas for review and they will lose influence with the group once it is obvious they do not have something positive to offer.

- I understand you don't support this program. What do you propose as an alternative? (The negative person may say he or she doesn't have a plan yet, but would like time to think about it.) Do you think we should continue with the meeting or delay it until you are ready? (He or she will probably let you continue.)
- You seem to be quite unhappy with how things are going. Do you want to take over the meeting and lead the brainstorming session to formulate the action plan?

**Note:** I've never known any negative person to accept this challenge. It opens them up to criticism, which negative people can rarely handle. They feel comfortable only on the edge making remarks.

# Chapter 9
# Generating Group Support
# for Meaningful Action

Meetings are held for a reason, and most often it is to create action of some sort—encouraging people to keep up the work, taking action to correct problems, or take a new turn in a company. In Chapter 8 we discussed getting general input from all the participants, but holding down long discussions from any one person. Now you have to cut the conversation and move into an action mode of creating a plan, proposal, or response relevant to your topic.

## Building Group Buy-in for an Action Plan

You are not in the same position to dictate the action plan as a supervisor is. You need to work on action much more as a team player, especially if some of the input has come from people who are your superiors. Your objective coming into the meeting is to get movement in what you perceive to be a positive direction, and not necessarily to have the group adopt your exact proposal. No matter how the final course is determined, you want group buy-in for some positive action.

### IF THE GROUP ACCEPTS YOUR PROPOSAL

If the group adopts your plan, you still want to be careful to act as a humble member of the group, and not someone who is scoring points.

- The consensus seems to be to go with my proposal. I really appreciate the support of the group on this proposal. Prior to the meeting many of you offered me your input about the proposal and I feel this is a real group effort. We all are going to have to pitch in to make this happen and it is a good starting point to have your buy-in.

- I feel the group is ready to buy into the original proposal which was put together with the help of [your supervisor] and [list others who helped]. We won't achieve our goals without full support, so I'm pleased everyone is able to get behind this action plan.

## IF YOUR PROPOSAL IS MODIFIED BASED ON GROUP INPUT

The best way to generate buy-in is to acknowledge that you have modified the action you hoped for at the meeting and have accepted the group's suggestions. You should take this tack even when the group's modifications are minor. Start both of these responses by stating, "From what I'm hearing, the group appears to favor [action supported by group]."

■ I feel that the changes suggested have made our response more effective and more acceptable to the other groups that will be involved. I'm firmly behind what appears to be the group consensus and, unless there are any serious objections, I think we should lay out our implementation plan.

■ I feel very good about the proposed action as it stands now with everyone's input. We still have to work out our implementation steps, both short and long term, and if I read the group correctly we are ready to move on to setting up a schedule or plan.

## IF SEVERAL ACTION PLAN PROPOSALS ARE ON THE TABLE

A peer-led meeting often will generate several plan proposals, often strongly advocated by individuals or factions. Since you need to follow a single course, you have to force the group to decide. You won't necessarily have strong group buy-in if you (or your supervisor) pick and choose parts of each plan. So put the onus of compromise on the people making the proposals. If you have many proposals, first narrow down the choices to two to discuss or, if there are just a few, to one. In either case, allow the participants to add parts of other plans. Stress your need to have a plan at the end of the meeting, to force a decision.

■ With our time frame, we need to come forward with one plan. I'd like to have you narrow the choice down to two and then have a short discussion. Before we vote, think about the proposal you favor and consider adding features from other proposals that you feel will strengthen your plan and help it gather more support.

■ Again, I know that forcing a decision on this topic is difficult, as we have a wide range of opinions. But we are in a position where doing nothing is far worse. We have two proposals, and I feel we must decide or the rest of the organization will feel we are ineffective. [Chief advocates], you have taken the lead on the two proposals on the table. Let's take a five-minute break. Can you talk with your supporters and choose a final proposal you'd like to offer the group before we decide? You might want to add some points from other plans to increase your support.

■ It appears there is too much dissension to make a decision today. I'll get together with [your supervisor] and [other important stakeholder] and select three or four people to act as the representatives for the group and elect an action. There is no way the task force will find an action that will keep everyone happy, but without a consensus I don't know how else we can proceed.

# Soliciting Individual Commitments

For a successful meeting, you need commitments to action. As a peer or a subordinate, you're not in a strong position to demand a commitment. You have to rely on the support of the stakeholder who put you in charge of the meeting and also on the fact that your final report might be read widely in the organization. I've attended many meetings in which the meeting leader failed to seek commitments, often to avoid confrontation, and the implementation plan failed.

## SOFTENING THE TONE OF THE REQUEST FOR COMMITMENT

You are not any participant's supervisor, so you can't seem to be too demanding personally, but you can add pressure for commitments by telling people you've been charged with preparing an action plan, proposal, or some other response to be distributed to your supervisor and other interested stakeholders.

- I need to prepare a report for [supervisor or other stakeholder(s)] on what action we are taking and who is responsible. Let me just go over the commitments I believe have been given so far. At the end you can tell me the commitments I've missed or if you can add any to my list.

- Thank you all for your help. My notes are a little sketchy. I'd appreciate it if you could each list your action items so I can include them in the final report.

## CHALLENGING THE EXTENT OF THE COMMITMENT

My experience is that when you are not the boss, you will get commitments that are convenient for the participants rather than effective for your project, response, or plans. You can't really go back and force a higher commitment, but you can ask, in a nonthreatening way, for a little more support.

- One of the goals of the meeting was to [specify action needed]. I'm concerned that the commitments we have so far won't be enough. Are we sure that the actions we have mentioned will enable us to achieve our goal? Or does anyone have something more to offer to strengthen our proposal?

- My initial reaction is that we just don't have enough impact with the commitments each of you have made. There are a couple of additional steps I can take—[list them]—but I'm still not sure that will be enough. Are there any more actions that any of you could offer, or any actions you are offering, that you could increase?

## ASKING FOR ADDITIONAL HELP AND COMMITMENT

When you run a meeting as a peer or a subordinate, you must constantly try to prevent the meeting from becoming a free-for-all. When you try to control the conversation, you run the risk of cutting off a creative solution or action that could really improve the meeting's results. Once you have commitments to make a solution possible, you should ask for any ideas for a creative response.

- I know we've kept our meeting on a tight schedule and, as a result, most of the suggestions and commitments have followed our more traditional response to similar situations. We still have some time left. Does anyone have any suggestions that offer a new twist?

- We have room to add to our proposal some new tactics that we may have never used before. We have a solid plan, so I think it might be a good idea to try out some innovative tactics. If they don't work, we should still be able to get by with the action and commitments we have now.

## Confirming the Action Plan Schedule

Without commitments and a schedule, you run the risk that participants will neglect to take action after the meeting.

### CHECKING FOR MISSING ITEMS

I can guarantee you will miss items, no matter how carefully you keep your list and how many times you read through it. So after preparing the rough draft, ask participants if you've missed any items. Then do this again with an e-mail follow-up.

- I have a feeling that we've left something off of the list. Does anyone see any items that we have overlooked?
- I feel a little blurry-eyed and I'm worried I'm not quite seeing straight. Can you all take just one last look at our action plan and see if there are any items I've missed?

### CHECKING FOR CONFLICTS

Your project, proposal, or plan is just one of probably dozens kicking around the organization. You want to be careful that your timing does not conflict with another project, proposal, or plan. If there's a conflict, people who have committed to take action might not be able to honor their commitments—especially if the other project, proposal, or plan is spearheaded by someone with more clout in the company.

- I know there are several key programs in progress right now or close to starting, some of them run by people higher up in the company than I. I don't want to be caught by surprise if any of you can't meet your commitment due to a conflict with another developing project. So please check your calendars to be sure that you aren't involved in another project that will create a scheduling problem for you.

- This response is important to me, but I know all of you are involved with other projects that are just as important. Do any of you see any conflicts that will make it impossible to complete your commitments?

# Chapter 10
# Dealing with Difficulties

Chapters 6 through 9 offer perfect phrases for meetings that are proceeding reasonably well and in which the participants are generally cooperative. This is not always the case. Some participants won't support an action and may even oppose it, others will just be difficult, and still others will not want to expend any effort to help you. As a peer, you don't have the power to enforce your will, but you still have three tactics to use:

- Using the support of superiors or stakeholders
- Cutting people out of the decision-making process
- Relying on the power of reports and follow-up to influence participants

You might have noticed that there are two tactics I don't list—confronting difficult participants and being nice. Confrontation might work on some people, but it will only generate resistance from many others. Niceness also may work with a few people, but that is not nearly enough to get most people moving forward, especially if they don't agree with you.

# Working with Participants Opposed to the Action Plan

Participants may have valid concerns about a proposal. Sometimes they may feel the drawbacks are greater than the others feel, sometimes the action may affect their area negatively, and sometimes they really just don't want to do anything. If you don't have any support, you may need to thank the group and then try to come up with a different approach and possibly call another meeting in a few weeks. But if you have support from at least half the participants, you probably will want to move forward.

## CLOSING OFF THE DISCUSSION AND MOVING FORWARD

You have already given the group a chance to offer options (see Chapter 9) and then had the participants, or maybe a supervisor, choose the action plan to pursue. With firm resistance, you need to work extra hard to get past this point.

- I know some of you are unhappy about the actions we are proposing to take. I know this proposal doesn't spread the pain and the gain evenly. Some people will make out much better than others. But our other alternative is to do nothing and that is not a choice many others in the organization will accept. This action plan will clearly fail if the people who don't support it refuse to participate. We need for all of us to do everything we can to make the plan work.

- I think we all agree the plan has flaws and doesn't work for everyone. Some of our concerns may not be well founded and we may be totally missing other issues that might develop into problems. We don't know. Let's run with the proposal for three months and then meet again to see how we can tweak the program or, if necessary, totally overhaul it or even scrap it. But we won't know how to evaluate the program unless we all put our best effort into implementing it.

## NOTING OPPOSITION

Participants may resist and not help to implement the action selected by the group. You can usually dissipate resistance if you note any opposition in reports so the opponents know their views were heard. Be careful to do this in a non-threatening manner or the opposition may stiffen.

- I understand that you are opposed to the action. If you'd like, I'm willing to note that in our meeting notes and also the summary report I'll prepare as a record of the meeting for circulation. Would you like me to do that?

- I don't want to imply in the meeting notes and report that we all support the direction we are taking, as that is clearly not the case. I thought I'd note in the report that you prefer [specify action]. Is that OK with you?

## USING THE THREE TACTICS

### 1. Using Support of Superiors or Stakeholders (if Attending)

- [Superior or stakeholder], you've heard some other points of view on our proposed response. Do you feel we should still continue with the plan?

**2. Removing People from the Decision-Making Process**

■ The group here doesn't appear to be making much progress, since we have several points of view. Since we need to create action, I think we might be better off if we go with a smaller task force of people who favor [state action].

**3. Relying on the Power of Reports and Follow-up**

■ We will have to scale back our implementation plan, with only those people who have been willing to commit to action. I'll just note in my report that the others at the meeting would not commit to action because they do not support the proposal.

## Overcoming a Lack of Commitment

A frequent problem with meetings is that the participants are not willing to commit to enough action to adequately resolve the issue that the meeting is addressing. They may be too busy or just unwilling to take on more assignments. Sometimes, their resistance to your plan also plays a part in their lack of commitment. You can explain in a report that you don't have the support required to meet the goal. However, first try to encourage commitment. Put all the facts on the table at the meeting and the participants may respond by increasing their support.

### SCALING BACK THE GOALS

You started the meeting with goals and objectives. If you believe that you can't achieve those goals with the commitment offered, you need to state clearly what you can accomplish, both during the meeting and later in your reports. When you broach this topic, list the less ambitious goals to get more attention.

- My take on where we stand right now is that we aren't going to hit our goals at this commitment level. Unless someone strongly disagrees, I believe we should let people know what goals we can hit with our commitments. Right now I'm ready to report that the goals we can achieve are [list reduced goals conservatively]. Does anyone disagree?
- I think the most important thing I'll need to do is report that the only goal the group can commit to is [specify conservative goal]. People won't be able to count on us achieving [state original goal]. I think it's better to disap-

point people now, rather than later. Does anyone have any objection to this approach?

## STATING CONSEQUENCES OR NEED FOR ALTERNATIVE ACTION

When your group fails to produce action plans and make commitments necessary to achieve their goals, there are typically consequences throughout the organization. You want to list the decisions of your meeting in a report to other groups that may need to take corrective action as a result of your meeting. The thought of going public with an inadequate response that will make your group look bad may motivate participants to increase their commitment.

- Since we aren't going to have much impact on this issue, I think it would be only fair to let others know that their areas may be negatively affected by our response and that their groups might want to form action committees to address the issue.

- I've made a short list of people I want to alert to our inability to respond aggressively to this issue, so they can determine what direction they want to take. So far I've put on my list [groups and supervisors]. Do you have other names you want to add to my list?

## USING THE THREE TACTICS

### 1. Using Support of Superiors or Stakeholders

- [Superior or stakeholder if not attending] was fairly adamant that we move in the necessary direction with momentum. He/she made it clear to me that this was a priority. I'll have to let him/her know we don't have enough commitment from the group to generate the momentum he wanted.

## 2. Removing People from the Decision-Making Process

■ I'm not ready to submit what we have committed to today. I'll meet with [superior or other stakeholder], explain where we are today, and then see what he/she wants to do. I expect he/she will want to look at your priorities and commitments and request certain actions from all or some of you. I'll keep you posted on what is finally decided.

## 3. Relying on the Power of Reports and Follow-up

■ I'll prepare a report of the commitments you've been able to make. Since I expect people to be disappointed, I'll also list the reasons, be they other priorities or your current workload, that each of you have given to justify why you cannot do more. Hopefully this will be enough for people to let this project go; otherwise we may need to meet again.

# *Part Three*

## *Attending Meetings as a Supervisor*

Y ou may not be leading the meeting, but everyone will still be expecting you to take a leadership role. The success or failure of any meeting you attend will be, at least in part, attributed to you. So you need to find a way to keep meetings going in a positive direction. You are especially on the spot when your direct reports lead the meeting, which is why you would be wise, if one of your subordinates is leading a meeting, to go over the agenda, objectives, and any presentations prior to the meeting.

You also have the challenge of helping the meeting move forward without appearing to stifle input from the participants. You need to master the art of giving every person the opportunity to have the others hear and appreciate his or her views even if the group doesn't adopt any suggestions offered.

# Chapter 11
# Ensuring a Productive Meeting

I read an article in the newspaper recently about how people like to attend meetings because they enjoy the social interaction. Well, if you are a supervisor, you clearly do not want your meetings to become social events. But a social-interaction meeting is not the worst thing that can happen; a meeting could degenerate into a verbal tussle in which participants choose sides or, worse, a battle in which participants play the blame game or enter into a shouting match.

## Reinforcing a Positive Tone

Many people need between three and ten positive experiences to feel like the meeting was successful. Even if the meeting ends up without any action or in an agreement between two factions to disagree, you still need the overall tone of the meeting to be positive.

## PRESENTING A BROADER PERSPECTIVE

The meeting leader and probably most of the participants will be looking at the agenda and the meeting objectives from the narrow perspective of how the issues affect them. That can often lead the participants to focus on protecting their interests. They will feel more positive if you cast the meeting as a part of the organization's overall objectives with a few initial comments right after the meeting leader's opening.

- This issue is creating some initial conflict because it takes us all outside our comfort zone, beyond the ways we've done things in the past. But one of our objectives is to grow 20 percent this year. That won't happen without dramatic change in how we do things. We all need to leave our comfort zone and adapt in order to hit the organizational goal. So when we discuss this topic, let's not think of what we'd like to see happen from our individual perspectives, but instead let's focus on the organizational objectives and how we can help achieve them.

- Our results are down 30 percent in the last five years. I know we'd all like to attribute that decline to external factors beyond our control, but we have to accept that some of our decline is the result of us not wanting to change and adjust to our changing environment. I think we have to look not at incremental change, but at shifting our entire outlook.

## HELPING OUT WHEN THINGS START GETTING UGLY

You can use comments from a broader perspective, if participants are simply protecting their territory. But the differences can go deeper and people can get passionate about promoting their views. You have to cut them off before they become too entrenched. This can usually be done by asking questions that make the person realize he or she is treading on dangerous ground.

■ Are you saying that there is nothing your group can do that would help?

■ Am I to understand that you feel you bear no responsibility for what has happened?

■ Do you feel the opposing point of view—[specify]—has no merit?

■ Why do you feel you know more about what customers want than the sales department?

■ Do you believe we have such a lock on the truth that we don't even need to consider a fresh perspective from an outside source?

## FINDING A POSITIVE NOTE WHEN THERE IS NO AGREEMENT

Some meetings do not reach a resolution, for any of various reasons. But you should not let a meeting end without some positive actions or the organization can slip into a mode of never getting things done. Instead, suggest actions that will remedy the situation for the next meeting.

- Let's have each group designate a person to spend 20 hours with the other group over the next month so we can all better understand each other's positions. Then let's have those two people prepare an action plan for a meeting in about six weeks.

- These conflicts seem pretty significant and I don't think we can resolve them today. I'd like to have a small task force of three or four people work together to try to find common ground over the next three months so we can move ahead.

## Clarifying Expectations for the Meeting

One of the more important responsibilities of a supervisor at a meeting is to keep the participants aware that meetings are more than just discussions of specific topics. They represent greater organizational goals and provide opportunities for participants to show they can compromise on issues. This longer-term vision can keep meetings from degrading into petty arguments.

### STRESSING THE BROADER GOALS

In the previous section of this chapter, I discussed a broader perspective in setting a positive tone. You also need to tie that broader goal into the expectations for this meeting, in effect making the meeting more important. Make these comments at the beginning of the meeting or at a time during the during the meeting when discussion bogs down.

- Our organization needs to achieve [objective] over the next six months. Right now [topic of meeting] is one of only four initiatives that can help us hit that goal. The pressure is on our group to respond with a program that produces the high impact necessary.

- I look at our agenda today as the first small task that sets off a domino effect. We have three tasks to accomplish in order to hit the first quarter goal of [be specific]. Before we can start those tasks, we need to clear this item off the agenda. So, while this topic might not at first glance seem important, it plays a key role in how all of us will be judged against our overall goals.

## EMPHASIZE THE VALUE OF WORKING TOGETHER

Meetings are not stand-alone events: they typically involve groups that need to meet at least somewhat frequently to advance the organization's goals. Cooperation and compromise are keys to a group's long-term success. Don't make these comments at the beginning, but use them at a time when the meeting loses mementum.

- All of us meeting here today form a key core group for creating positive change in the organization. We will be addressing over the next 12 months many controversial issues that will generate radically different ideas among us. We need to look at each meeting as a part of a longer process in which, in order to be effective, we all must be very cooperative.

- Our group here today is one of the three major action groups in the organization. To keep up with the other groups, we are going to have to work together to make sure each meeting creates a meaningful action that will contribute toward achieving our organization's goals.

## STATING THE OPTIMUM RESULT

I've found it effective to state what would be the best outcome for a meeting in terms of the organization. That result is almost never achieved, but it pushes meeting participants to respond at a higher level than they would otherwise.

- I believe that everyone in the organization will be pleased if this meeting results in [action] I don't know if we will get to that point, but let's all work together to come as close to that goal as possible.

- I'm hoping that from this meeting, we can show management that we have a real chance of hitting our targets next year. To do that I feel we are going to need to develop a realistic plan for [topic] at today's meeting.

## Clarifying Expectations for the Participants

Effective supervisors constantly keep the bar high for their subordinates and others in the organization. You can do that in your day-to-day activities, but I've found that meetings are especially effective opportunities to reinforce the message that you have high expectations.

### CHALLENGING THEIR PRECONCEPTIONS

Most meetings have agenda items that are familiar to all participants; in fact, in most cases the participants will already have some firmly entrenched views on some or all agenda items and the actions to be taken. Meetings can be unproductive if the participants refuse to move from these views.

- I know most of you have your own views of this topic. But we are meeting because we haven't moved forward yet. There may be many reasons for this lack of progress, but one may be that our entrenched perspectives just don't work anymore. I feel we will have a better chance of making progress if we forget about our preconceptions and keep our minds open during the meeting.

- We've met on this topic before and we hit a brick wall, primarily, in my opinion, because our preconceptions have kept us from seeing others' points of view. I firmly believe we can find a compromise if we all just keep our minds open and try to understand what each of us is really saying.

### CONTRIBUTING PROPORTIONATELY TO THE FINAL ACTION

Rarely does any action item divide the work up evenly, which could be due to job responsibilities, differences in experience and abilities, or time commitments. But action after meetings tends to slow down or participants tend to become resentful if they do not all share in the plan somewhat in proportion to their responsibilities and abilities.

■ I'm hoping that whatever action the group decides today will represent a team effort, with every member contributing whatever he or she can in line with his or her abilities and responsibilities.

■ I'll be disappointed if the meeting ends up putting a big burden on just a few members of our group. I'm hoping for some real momentum to come out of this meeting. I don't see how we can create that momentum unless every one of us contributes to the effort.

## CARRYING OUT RESPONSIBILITIES FROM THE MEETING

Meetings will be judged by the actions and responses they generate. Effective meetings have an impact on the organization only if people accept and carry out their responsibilities from those meetings. As a rule you get the results you want only by letting the people responsible for actions know that you are closely tracking their progress.

■ I've asked [meeting organizer or another interested party] to keep track of your commitments today and to follow up with each of you every two weeks to see that all of us are on target to fulfill our responsibilities.

■ I'd like each of you to give me a biweekly update on your progress or include the update in your weekly activity reports.

# Chapter 12
# Clarifying and Framing
# the Meeting Issue

As a supervisor, you want meetings to support your agenda and the direction you want your department to take. The easiest way to do this is to control how the issue is presented. That allows you to steer the meeting and frame the issues in a favorable direction.

Politicians do this all the time. For example, politicians who want to limit the number of illegal immigrants will want to evaluate proposals in terms of amnesty for illegal activities and argue that amnesty is wrong. Politicians who want to support immigrants in the country will talk in terms of family units; they will want to evaluate any proposal in terms of what it does to families and argue that it is wrong to destroy family units.

When you control how an issue is framed, you can control how the issue is discussed, which will help move the decision in the direction you want. You should clarify how an issue is defined even if you don't have a preferred course of action, as doing so will help keep the group discussing the issue from a shared perspective. Otherwise, it is unlikely you will end up with a consensus. You should do this at the start of the meeting. It offers you the best chance—first, to generate a meaningful discussion and second, to steer the discussion toward your goals.

## Framing the Issue from Your Point of View

I've found that most people have a way they would like to consider an issue, but they don't know how to frame that issue in a statement that communicates their views effectively to the group in a way that can move the discussion forward. You might want to meet briefly with the meeting leader, especially if he or she is a subordinate, to ensure that how this issue is framed doesn't hinder achieving his or her goals. If you succeed in framing the discussion from your point of view, the meeting will usually go your way.

Here's an example of framing an issue. The service department calls a meeting to decide how to allow employees to take their vacation time in a way that will not disrupt company–customer service levels. The service department manager might want to shut down for two weeks because it is too difficult to ensure proper service with limited resources. That might be true, but stating the issue in those terms, which in effect imply the job is too tough, suggests that the manager is unable to handle the situation. So the manager might frame the issue as "How do we guarantee 100 percent quality service with two thirds of the staff at any one time over the summer?" Now the department is focusing the discussion on something that all of the parties want—high quality control—and can build momentum in the discussion.

## DECIDING WHAT'S GOOD AND WHAT'S BAD

Defining an issue in a favorable way is not always easy. You should start by listing the factors you consider good and the factors you consider bad.

- In our example, the service provider group, which wants to shut down for two weeks, lists as good factors high-quality service and minimum disruption—two to three weeks if it shuts down versus 12 weeks with two-thirds staffing if it remains open. It also lists as bad factors that customers would go for two weeks without service and the company would develop a service backlog.

An alternative framing of this issue, possibly by the sales and marketing department, which wants the service department to stay open, might be that the company can't afford to lose customers who would be unable to get service if the service department is shut down. The good factor is that the company is doing everything it can to protect its top customers and the bad factor is that at two-thirds staffing either service might be spotty or second- and third-tier customers would have to wait for service.

## PROTECTING THE GOOD AND/OR ATTACKING THE BAD

You want to be prepared with short sound bites to promote your position. Sound bites work because they are easy to remember, but they still must make a point that everyone accepts. You have to be prepared with your position and comments from the beginning of the meeting or the participants might take on another reference point as the consensus viewpoint.

Protecting the good type of comments in our example could be:

- Our reputation has been built on our ability to deliver 100 percent quality (service department view).
- We need to protect our relationships with our top customers or we won't continue to grow (sales department view).

Attacking the bad type of comments in our example could be:

- Without a shutdown, we will be providing bad service for 12 to 14 weeks (service department view).
- Our customers will be crippled if our lack of service halts their production (sales department view).

## Questioning the Meeting Leader

The person leading the meeting has set an agenda and more than likely has given some indication of the issue. You need to clarify the issue as soon as the meeting starts.

For example, the meeting might be called because Customer X has stated that the products you are shipping do not meet its technical specifications. The issue for the meeting might be:

- Renegotiating the specifications
- Determining costs to meet the specifications
- Adding process inspection steps to meet the specifications
- Developing a short-term action plan to save the account
- Determining the organization's ability to respond to new standards
- Identifying process improvements necessary to meet the specifications

If you are the marketing and sales manager, the issue you might want to address is developing a short-term action plan to save that account. The production manager might want the issue to be defined as renegotiating the customer's specifications. You question the meeting leader to clarify the issue for the group, hopefully in a manner favorable to your perspective and interests.

## STATING THE ISSUE IN YOUR TERMS

Simply give your definition of the issue and then ask the person leading the meeting if that is correct. If you state the issue in a matter-of-fact manner, the leader probably will not feel as if you are challenging him or her.

- Is the goal of the meeting to determine how we can increase product deliveries to keep our position as the number-one supplier to [name of customer]?
- I'm not sure this came through in the agenda, but isn't one of our objectives to bring the [name of group or department] into the decision process?
- I came prepared to discuss how we can increase our use of customer feedback in developing our new services. Is that the direction we are headed?

## ASKING FOR A DEFINITION AND THEN ATTEMPTING TO MODIFY IT

Sometimes you aren't sure of the direction the meeting leader is going. In that case, rather than try to push your agenda, you might want first to check the intended direction and then to try to modify it.

- What is the one key question/problem/issue/action that you feel we will be discussing today? (If the answer is not what you want, follow up.) Don't you feel the question of [what you want] is just as important?
- What would you say would be the perfect result from our meeting? (If the answer is too broad, e.g., "a solution that makes everyone happy," follow up with a question to get more definition.) What type of solution do you think would be best? (If the answer is not what you want, follow up.)

Would you be willing to accept a totally different type of solution, for instance [your solution]?

## CHALLENGING THE ISSUE DEFINITION

Sometimes you can tell from the agenda or from memos related to the meeting that the meeting planner is not framing the issue in terms favorable to you. If you feel the soft approach won't work, you can be more direct and count on your position as supervisor to sway the group to the way you want to consider the issue.

- Can you explain to me why you're not framing the issue as [your perspective]? That seems like an approach that deals with the most important aspects of the situation.

- I thought you would approach this issue by considering [your perspective]. Why did you decide to look at the situation from a totally different point of view?

# Focusing the Presentation on the Issue

All topics have many facets that your group could consider. If you considered all of them, your meetings would go nowhere. I've found that successful meetings (and companies) concentrate on only the three or four points that have the most impact on the decision, topic, or response. You need to focus the discussion on the key issue and, if possible, your point of view on that issue.

## AIMING THE MEETING AT YOUR TARGET

Probably the most destructive activity in most meetings is discussing points that are relevant but not significant. A 60-minute presentation can be much worse than a ten-minute presentation if it brings up points that are not significant. Straying onto minor points may cause the participants to stray from the framework you want to use to discuss the issue. You want to keep the presentation focused on the points that you consider significant and you may need to be proactive to keep the presentation on target.

- I appreciate the points you are trying to make, but our first goal has to be to address [issue from your perspective].
  I think bringing up less important points at this time might keep us from finding a meaningful response.

- Let's try to stay focused on [issue from your perspective], unless you feel that another perspective on the issue is more important.

## CHALLENGING POINTS THAT CHANGE THE FRAMING OF THE ISSUE

It's generally difficult to keep a meeting focused on what is important from your point of view. People will bring up nuances, details, and minor points if you let them. You don't want to stifle meaningful conversation, but you want the participants to really consider what they are saying and refrain from saying whatever comes to their minds.

- Do you think that point has "top-three" significance in terms of this issue?
- I don't want to clutter up the discussion with too many considerations, many of which might be of only minor importance. Is there a point made earlier that you feel should be replaced by the point you just made?
- Why do you feel the point you've made should have a major influence on our decision process?
- Our goal here isn't to consider our decision from every possible angle. We want to consider it from only the important angles. Can you justify that point being one of those important angles?

# Chapter 13
# Group Reaction and Participation

Supervisors have four goals for meetings:

- Help the meeting reach its objective.\
- Ensure that all the participants feel that their views have been considered.
- Support the personal growth of the people who work for them.
- Show their leadership potential.

To achieve all four goals, you need to help all the other participants do well in the meeting and you need to move the group to accept your point of view without sounding like you are ordering the group into action. You also need to help the participants see beyond the immediate topic and understand how that topic is a part of the bigger picture of the organization's goals.

# Eliciting Contributions from All

The goal is to get a result that all the participants will support, even if they disagree. This happens only if they all feel they have had an opportunity to express their views. You also have to be careful that they don't perceive that you are favoring any person or group over any others. One way to avoid that perception to the extent possible, since no one is ever viewed as totally impartial, is to do your best to allow all the participants a reasonable amount of time to make their point.

## PROTECTING FREEDOM OF EXPRESSION

There will always be people who try to jump in to stifle comments from others, even comments that might support their point of view. You should be able to prevent such behavior effectively and with tact.

- Excuse me. I'd like to have [person interrupted] finish his/her comment. I believe his/her point might be one we all should hear.

- [Person interrupting], I know you are passionate about this. But we need to be careful not to be so passionate that we ignore other perspectives. We need to consider all points to be sure our passion is not misplaced.

## ASKING DIRECT QUESTIONS

Some people are intimidated by others in the group or they may defer to people whom they respect or with whom they work. I've found that a sequence of three questions works well to elicit contributions from quiet participants. A bonus of using this approach consistently is that you force participants to keep alert.

- [Person], what do you feel is the proper course for us to take?
- What are your top two reasons for wanting to follow that course?
- Can you offer any reasons that haven't already been mentioned?

## KEEPING A SCORECARD

This is useful if there are several prevailing points of view. Make a list of positive and negative aspects of each point of view. Ask each participant to list one reason, positive or negative, until all feel the list is complete. Using a scorecard allows you to get a better sense of where participants stand by their comments and it gives them all a chance to state their dominant thoughts on the issue.

- Let's list on the board our three top points of view and then list positive and negative factors for each. Let's go around the room and get one point at a time from each of you. That will help me get a better sense of how each of you feels.
- I'm going to make a little scorecard to show where we are so we can figure out where we are going. Let's go around the room a few times. I'd like you each to give one pertinent point—either positive or negative. Then, explain in one or two sentences why you feel it's important. When we are done, we can each rate which three points are most important to us. We can then limit our discussion to those points.

## Controlling the Dominators

Dominating people are often a problem, especially if they have been allowed to disrupt meetings in the past. You want to help the meeting leader control the dominators while still receiving their input. This is even more important if the dominators work for you.

As mentioned in previous chapters, four types of people try to dominate and disrupt meetings: bullies, prima donnas, passive-aggressive people, and overly negative people. (See Chapter 3 for descriptions of these four personalities.) You don't want to assume responsibility for controlling any dominators, since the person leading the meeting should be doing that, but you should help when needed.

### BULLIES

You definitely need to help if bullies attack the person leading the meeting, but you should also help if they are attacking someone else. A good way to neutralize bullies is to express concern that their attitude is a result of a hidden agenda.

- [Bully], your comments and attacking style are undermining the efforts of [leader]. Do you have a specific objection to this topic and proposed action that you would like to put on the table for the group's consideration?
- [Bully], why does the point [person attacked] is making disturb you so much? It seems like a valid point and one that I think we should consider. Do you have a specific reason for wanting to take this issue off the table?

## PRIMA DONNAS

The less experienced the person leading the meeting, the more likely a prima donna will try to impress everyone with his or her knowledge and expertise. The best sort of comments are ones that undermine the prima donna's feeling of superiority while reinforcing the point that input is needed from all participants.

- I was hoping that I could report to [stakeholder or another supervisor] that this group came up with a really innovative solution to this problem. But to do that, we cannot just try the first thing that comes to mind. Instead, we need to hear everyone's point of view. We should be open especially to new members of our group, who often see things in a different light than those of us who have been here for a while.
- I understand your position, but two heads are better than one and we have many heads here.
- By coming together and using everyone's observations, we will definitely develop a better solution than any one of us alone could propose.

## PASSIVE-AGGRESSIVE PEOPLE

When participants get away with little indirect digs, they can drag down the whole meeting. They have learned that they can get away with their remarks because they make them indirectly. They will usually stop when you address their remarks or their attitudes openly. Passive-aggressive people like to feel safe to make digs. Take away that feeling of security and they tend to be silent.

- [Passive-aggressive person], your comments are confusing me. Your words and voice tone and body language just don't match up. Could you make your future comments on point? Otherwise, you're a distraction in this meeting.
- Effective communication requires trust. Unfortunately, [passive-aggressive person], I don't trust what you're saying. I feel like you have an agenda behind your comments. Please keep in mind that this meeting and all of our other work require open and honest communication.

## OVERLY NEGATIVE PEOPLE

There are many reasons why people might be negative. Sometimes they don't want to change at all, other times they don't like a specific change, and sometimes they are just negative by nature. You can neutralize negative behavior by letting overly negative participants know that their negativism only makes them look bad.

- I believe success requires only 50 percent of your decisions to be correct. In most instances, the biggest mistake is to do nothing. [Negative person], you appear to be negative. Do you have a compelling reason not to move ahead?
- People who advance in the company look for ways to get things done despite any obstacles. When people don't try for a solution, they let the organization down. [Negative person], do you support what's being proposed or do you have another proposal you would like to throw on the table?

## Reinforcing the Leader and the Other Participants

This section isn't about telling people they've done a good job. It's about letting participants know that what they are doing is important to the organization.

As a rule, people won't be proactive or committed to a project unless they know or believe or hope it has some importance, either for themselves or for the organization. When the person running the meeting is one of your subordinates or has less experience, he or she may concentrate on the task at hand, so the responsibility of emphasizing the importance of the meeting will fall to you.

### CONCENTRATING ON THE KEY ISSUE

Meetings easily slip off target, stray into minutiae, or become a venue for personal squabbles. The way to get back on track is to reiterate the key issue for the meeting, not just the topic.

For example, the key issue for an order-tracking system might be that customer service cannot project a ship date, while the meeting might be about what features the new system should have. When the meeting slows down, remind the other participants that you are all meeting because customers cannot receive an accurate estimated ship date.

- This meeting feels like it's bogging down because we appear to be losing focus on why we are here. I'll just remind you that the issue that should be at the forefront is [key issue]. We need to make progress with that issue today.

■ Let's stop for a minute and focus on [key issue]. That's our real target here today. I'm beginning to worry that our discussion is addressing another concern and we are not putting together a plan for the right issue.

## SHOWING A CONNECTION TO THE BIG PICTURE

In my experience, between 70 and 90 percent of people attending meetings don't believe that what they can do will have a significant positive effect on the organization. People who think that way need to understand that their lack of action might hold back the organization. Those who already believe their actions can positively affect the organization just need to know they are working on a project that could help the organization achieve its goals.

■ This task might not seem to merit important consideration, but it works toward one of the organization's goals: [specify goal]. Our efforts here today will help pave the way for [specify project]. If we don't address this situation and take action, our group may be viewed as a roadblock.

■ I feel today like a doorkeeper. We need to open the door so the rest of the organization can rush in and work on [goal]. If we fail, people will be pacing, frustrated, and even angry. I realize that, if we succeed, others may not even notice our efforts. But they will notice for sure if we don't eliminate this obstacle.

## EXPLAINING THE IMPORTANCE OF THE GOAL OF A MEETING

Sometimes a meeting is about an important goal and many in the organization will be noticing the results. Explaining to the group why the goal is important will keep the members focused and motivated.

- The organization has trusted this group to achieve significant progress today on [topic]. Our efforts today will represent a key step toward the organization's goal of [specify]. People throughout our organization are interested in our progress today. I will be disappointed if we can't report, at least, that we are off to a good start.

- Most of us play a supporting role to other groups in a position to try to resolve some problem. That is not the case today. We are at the leading edge, working toward the organization's goal of [specify]. Now other groups are supporting us. I believe it will behoove all of us to raise our performance level.

# Chapter 14
# Changing the Action Plan
# to Meet Your Goals

A good supervisor is one who excels because of the performance of his or her staff. A good supervisor encourages his or her people to take a lead role and feel fully involved in the decision-making process.

I feel it is always smart to give meaningful consideration to the input of every meeting participant: you can often gain insights you might have overlooked, the participants feel more confident that they're contributing, and, most important, it is the best way to encourage participants to buy into the action plan. However, there are times when you need to modify the actions they are proposing. You can still adjust the plans even though you're not leading the meeting, as long as you can do it diplomatically.

## Stating Your Position Clearly

Whether or not you agree with the proposal or perspective being discussed, your best course is to clearly state your position at that point in the meeting. If the group consensus is close to yours, you are ready to move on to the action phase. If it is not the same or similar, you should give the group an opportunity, if possible, to consider your position in developing its strategy, rather than attempting to use your supervisory position to request a change in direction. My experience is that if the members of a group respect the supervisor, they will readily adapt to his or her position.

### YOU AGREE WITH THE GROUP

You should compliment the group and state that you agree with its decision process and you are ready to move on to the action plan. Do not take credit for the decision, but also do not imply that you are simply going along with the group's decision. (After all, other times you will not go along with the group's decisions.) Just state that you agree with this decision.

- The group seems to have reached the position that [state position]. I like this position. My reasoning is slightly different, as I place more emphasis on [cite a relevant factor], but your reasons are just as valid.

- Good comments from everybody! I agree with the group's consensus that we should [state consensus]. This decision certainly meets our objective today of [specify] as well as being in sync with the organizational goal(s).

## YOU DISAGREE WITH THE GROUP

If you did a good job framing the issue from your perspective (Chapter 12), the participants will already know the direction in which you are leaning and should have already tried to adjust their views so they can at least coexist with yours. But that doesn't always happen. If you state your views clearly now, you can offer the group another chance to adjust its consensus so that it supports yours.

■ I appreciate the effort and thought you've put into this issue today, but my position on this issue doesn't line up with yours. I feel [state your position]. Is there some way we can keep some of the good thoughts you have put forward but still support my position?

■ My position is [state your position]. I know my views have come out in the discussion and some of you have supported my position, but not all of you. I'm not ready to give it up, though, because [one or two reasons for your position]. I don't want to discount your opinions, but I feel my position is best for the organization. Is there a way we can modify the group's position so we can all be happy?

## Adjusting for the Group's Consensus

The reality is that the group members will work much harder to act on a plan that they believe is theirs than to support a plan you force on them. If you disagree with a position the group is taking during a meeting, compare your position and the group's and be sure that yours is better before trying to persuade the group to buy in further. This is true if the participants are your direct reports, but even more so if the participants do not report to you. In the latter case, you must work even harder to turn the meeting in your direction.

### YOU ARE ABLE TO ACCEPT THE CONSENSUS

You may believe that the group's position represents a viable option or its action plan won't cause any harm and you are not under any pressure to push a particular course of action. In these cases, you might want to concede to the group. Also a veiled challenge to prove you wrong can be a very effective motivator.

■ You've chosen a course that is different from the course I would have chosen, but I can't see any reason why it won't work, so I'll support your efforts. I'm counting on the group to come through on this, so you must work together. I'm looking forward to following this project as it progresses.

■ You all seem convinced that your action plan will work and that it will meet our targets. The whole organization is counting on your judgment and experience, which must be reflected in your approach to this problem. Be sure to get together over the next few weeks to talk about your progress to be sure you're doing everything necessary.

## YOU WANT TO INSIST ON YOUR POSITION

You may be under pressure from other stakeholders for a certain action. The issue involved may be so important you want to take a course that is less risky than the course proposed by the group. You may feel sure that your approach is significantly better. You have the managerial prerogative of insisting on your way if the group members are your direct reports, or if you have the support of all the members' supervisors. If you decide to insist, do it carefully.

- I think that the points presented are good, but I just don't feel comfortable with that course of action. I'd much prefer that we [state action you want]. I know this action is not what you prefer, but I need everyone to get behind it now and make sure we can successfully execute it.

- Your strategy has a lot of merit, but it is not one that I'm going to be able to approve. I don't feel it will satisfy the other stakeholders and I do not feel they are likely to compromise on this issue. I know that you do not agree, but I think we need to go with the actions we know others will accept.

## Returning Control to the Meeting Leader

Once you have made your position known, you should allow the leader to resume running the meeting. The leader may have retained control of the meeting and simply included your comments in the discussion. If not, the leader may quickly take charge again when your intervention ends. But the meeting may be "stuck in dead space." If so, it will be up to you to normalize the meeting.

### WHEN THE LEADER HAS EXPERIENCE

The leader will be able to resume control without much trouble as long as you make it clear that's what you expect. You can add a comment about the importance of the issue and/or the performance of the leader.

- [Leader], I apologize for taking over. I didn't mean to do that, but I feel this topic is important and I want us to create a plan that will keep all our stakeholders happy. Go ahead with your agenda.

- [Leader], I jumped in here more than I'd planned. You were doing a great job. I'll just stop talking, and you can get us back on track to finish on time.

### WHEN THE LEADER HAS LESS EXPERIENCE

Sometimes a leader not accustomed to running a meeting may stumble a bit when you return the meeting to him or her. You can help the leader by giving specific instructions for proceeding.

- [Leader's name], sorry for taking over for you there for a few minutes. Since we've decided on our response, why don't you ask for input for an action list, and the names of the people to whom we should send our response, and the times by which we should do so? This would also be a good time for you to ask about who should notify any stakeholders who require a personal contact.
- [Leader], I think I got a little carried away there, but I think we are ready for you to start our action plan. Let's put together two action plans—short and long. Maybe you could start by getting the group's input on what actions should be in our short-term plan and then follow up by getting commitments for those actions.

## Ensuring That the Group Is Prepared to Execute the Plan

Even when people meet with the best intentions and develop an action plan together, it often happens that the plan to which they commit remains only a plan. The meeting leader, if he or she is a peer of the participants, may not be able to hold them to their commitments. Two ways to help participants follow through on their commitments are by letting them know you are tracking their progress or by asking them for progress reports.

### WHEN YOU SENSE DISSENSION

In these cases, you need to upgrade your tracking system, but you want to do this without causing the participants to feel like you don't trust them to perform. Instead, ask for tracking so you or the meeting leader can prepare a report for the stakeholders or other people in the organization.

- I appreciate everyone's support on our response (or "action plan" or other meeting outcome), even though I know some of you would have preferred a different course. I'm asking [leader] for a biweekly report that I can pass on to other interested people in the organization.

- Our response looks very solid and should satisfy our stake-holders (specify). I'm preparing an action list for reports I'll be sending out, so e-mail me any additional actions you are planning and I'll include them on the list. I'll follow up with each of you every two weeks to see where we stand.

## WHEN THE GROUP SHOWS TEPID SUPPORT

You need to be very wary of lukewarm support; it is even worse than disagreement, because at least people who disagree show interest in the issue. I feel you need to be emphatic to make sure that the group members realize you'll be monitoring their performance. You don't have to worry about offending them; you need to light a fire under them to get them motivated.

■ I don't sense much enthusiasm about this topic. I'm disappointed, because this project is important to the organization as it targets the goal of [be specific]. Frankly, I'm worried you aren't going to give this your best effort and that's something I cannot tolerate. I'll need biweekly status reports from each of you, starting [date].

■ I need all of you to do some attitude adjustment here and generate some real energy for this project. We need to get it done and we need to do it really well or our group's image is going to suffer within the organization. We have a chance to stand out here, as people will be monitoring our results. [Meeting leader] will contact you in a week for your updated plan and then track your results over the next three months.

# Chapter 15
# Dealing with Difficulties

When a meeting goes bad, as they sometimes do, everyone looks bad—but especially the supervisors and particularly whichever supervisor has the highest standing in the organization. Supervisors are expected to be able to bail out a meeting that has gone astray. Being able to do that shows real leadership. But your responsibility is still to do what is best for the organization, which means that meeting participants often don't get what they want—and sometimes are extremely disappointed.

# Softening the Impact of Rejection on the Leader

Good supervisors provide their employees the freedom to come up with their own initiatives. That is the best way to encourage forward momentum in the group. If you allow freedom of action and encourage initiative, you will be attending meetings where you or the other members of the group don't blindly support the proposal of the person leading the meeting but work together to find the the best solution instead. If you want to continue to encourage initiative, you must soften the impact of that rejection on the leader and help him or her accept the decision of the other members of the group not to adopt the proposal that he or she has presented.

## POINTING OUT THE POSITIVES

All new initiatives and proposals have some value, even when they are turned down. They may bring out another perspective on an issue, they may highlight market information of which the group was unaware, and they may pinpoint trends or events that bear watching in the future. Those are positives that help your organization in the long term.

- [Leader], you may be ahead of the curve here. Your presentation was helpful, as it brought out issues that we haven't examined yet. Although we're not ready to move ahead today, your presentation will help us view the organization's activities in a new light. Maybe we will be ready for your proposal in another six to twelve months.

- [Leader], you've done us a service here. We haven't reviewed this procedure for at least three years and it appears that we may need to upgrade it, although not to the extent you propose. We should really evaluate all of our long-standing policies every 12 to 24 months.

## GENERATING AN EXPLORATORY ACTION PLAN

Often, new initiatives falter because there is not enough information to support them. The presenter might also highlight certain areas related to the issue but ignore others that you or other group members feel are pertinent. You might not be able to support the change now, but you might want to support further exploration.

- ■ I still find this concept intriguing and think that we should investigate this further. [Leader], let's get together over the next few days and put together a plan for exploring this issue a little more. This is an issue we definitely might want to revisit.

- ■ [Leader], have you talked with anyone else in the group about your idea? (If yes, talk with that other person.) [Other person], would you be willing to work with [leader] to put together a plan for how we can gather some of the information we're missing?

## SUPPORTING PARTS OF A PROPOSAL

Maybe the whole proposal won't make sense or have group support, but you can still salve the leader's wounds by picking a part of his or her proposal to implement. That shows you find some merit in the proposal and you're still supporting and encouraging the person.

- ■ [Leader], while the total package appears to be going too far too fast, I think some of your points show merit. Would you be willing to put together a less ambitious proposal with the items that had support? I don't think there is a need to meet again, but let me see what you put together and we perhaps can move forward with that.

- Like the other members of the group, I was surprised by the scope of the program. But we can't just decide not to explore intriguing ideas because they are new. [Leader], is there anyway we can set up a trial program so we can try out some of your ideas and see where they take us?

## Overcoming a Lack of Commitment

Both you and the organization have commitments and often, to meet your promises, you need support and strong commitments from others. Chapter 5 deals with overcoming a lack of commitment when you are in charge of the meeting. You can use those same tactics here, when one of your employees is leading the meeting, especially when the commitments needed reflect on your job performance. This section deals with situations in which the group fails to commit to the objectives of the meeting.

### CALLING ATTENTION TO THE LACK OF COMMITMENT

More inexperienced meeting leaders may not realize that the commitments they have received are just not enough to meet their objectives or they may just be optimistic that they can succeed with less than they really need. The first step to correct the situation is to help the leader recognize that he or she has a problem.

- [Leader], do you feel you have enough commitment from the group to hit your objective? (If yes) I'm not sure you can do it with the commitments you have. You need to go back to the group and see if you can get more support. (If no) I agree; we need people to step up and offer more.

- [Leader], I have an uncomfortable feeling that the support you have is going to leave you high and dry and unable to finish the job to anyone's satisfaction. I think you have to go back to the group and get more support.

**REQUESTING OTHER OPTIONS**

If people can't commit to the leader's plan enough to meet the objectives, maybe someone can suggest another way to approach the problem.

- With these commitment levels, this project will never work. We could kill the project, but then each of you would have to pick up the slack by improving performance in your areas and I don't know if any of you want to do that. What other options do we have to put on the table?
- Clearly this approach won't work. We just don't have the support we need. But we need to do something with impact. Let's brainstorm here and see what options we can find. Otherwise, we have to come back to this approach and find a way to make it work.

**REQUESTING A NEW PLAN**

Sometimes group members are not committing to a plan because they just don't support the ideas behind the plan. In that case, it might make more sense to consider developing another plan.

For example, an organization might be trying to grow by attacking a new market with its current products. But the group might disagree with this strategy, feeling that either new products are needed or other markets would be better. At a meeting called to determine how to hit second-quarter goals in the market, the group members will be unresponsive because they think the overall strategy is wrong.

- It looks like we are spinning our wheels and going nowhere. We need a 25 percent increase in performance this year. During our annual budget cycle last May, we decided that since our penetration was high in our current markets we needed to attack Market X. Now the group isn't willing to commit to hit our second-quarter goals, primarily because we have not met our targets in Market X. I'm getting the sense in this meeting today that you don't feel you can commit to sales in Market X. So I have a question: do you feel we are going after the wrong market or do you feel we have the wrong strategy for the market? If we have a basic flaw in our strategy, we need a new plan that will enable us to achieve 25 percent growth.

- I'm getting the feeling that the resistance to the issue today is coming from disagreement over some of our basic goals and strategies rather than the specifics we're discussing now. Otherwise, we should have already wrapped up our discussion by now. Can anyone fill me in on what broader issues are creating your resistance?

# Handling the Conclusion of a Murky Meeting

Despite all your best efforts, meetings do not always come to a nice clean conclusion. Maybe you're meeting with groups that won't go along with your plans. Maybe your goal is unachievable. Maybe participants will bring up valid objections that change your perspective, or that of the presenter or the meeting leader. That doesn't mean you should just leave on a down note, as if nothing can be done. Try to show how the meeting was still useful as it helped focus the group on working toward important goals.

## RETURNING TO THE ORGANIZATION'S GOALS

One of the reasons you stress the organization's goals is that those must be met. If you fail to generate momentum toward those goals at your meeting, you need to do something else to compensate. Otherwise, people who prefer inaction to action will look for ways to derail meetings.

■ This meeting ties into our overall goal of [state goal]. Unfortunately, this approach doesn't appear to answer all the questions, so we still must find ways to achieve this goal. Why don't you each send me one or two ideas for achieving this goal with another approach? Then we will meet next week to choose an action response.

■ OK, I know there was a mix of opinions today, but the result is not that we failed to make any progress. I'm looking for a response now as to what we will do instead to hit the broader objectives that were behind the meeting, which are [state objectives]. Within the next week, please,

I'd like each of you to send me a short, informal proposal for what we should do next.

## REMOVING OBSTACLES

Sometimes group members lose their enthusiasm and a meeting loses momentum because of a problem or an obstacle. For example, you might not want to move ahead because your plan might upset a key stakeholder, because you are not sure if another part of the organization can do certain tasks, or because you might not have enough people to execute the action plan. In this case, you should end the meeting by attacking those problems or obstacles so you can advance at the next meeting.

- We're not in a position to advance right now, but we have to keep focused on our goal of [state goal] and we need to keep working toward meeting that goal. I've listed five obstacles and problems that are slowing us down. I need each of you to pick one or two of these obstacles, do a quick evaluation, and then report back within one week with strategies for eliminating those obstacles.

- We talked about several concerns that have put this project on hold for the moment. Let's make a list of these concerns and categorize them as "must address," "better to address," and "can ignore." Once we understand the concerns, we can all volunteer to take on one or more of the obstacles so we can get back on course.

## FINDING WAYS TO WORK TOGETHER

You will be in many meetings that involve different groups, so you will not have control over all of the participants.

When others do not respond, you have a few tactics you can use for leverage. A tactic that typically works is to state that you need to find at least one way in which the groups can interact or else both or all groups look dysfunctional in their inability to fulfill the organization's goals.

- I don't want to report that our groups were unable to reach agreement on any meaningful issue. That doesn't help the organization at all. In fact, it makes it sound like our groups are dysfunctional. We must be able to find some area in which we agree to take action that will initiate at least some progress.

- Several of the organization's key goals will be in jeopardy if we can't compromise and achieve something here today. I'm wide open to any suggestions on how we can work together. I'm willing to try anything to avoid having to go back and tell the stakeholders that we couldn't find a way to cooperate.

# Part Four

## Attending Meetings with Peers and Superiors

A t most meetings you will be only a participant. The previous sections have concentrated on getting the results required as the meeting leader or the group's manager. In this section the focus is on how you can attend meetings, look like top management potential, protect your turf or responsibilities from encroachment, and avoid getting burdened with more assignments than you can handle.

There is a natural conflict between you and the meeting leader or your manager: they want to take your time and energy so they can achieve their goals, while you want to protect your time and energy so you can achieve your own goals. You need to protect your time and energy without appearing to be a complainer and while giving the impression you are a can-do, responsible person who knows how to handle people. All in all a pretty tall order—one that you can fill if you are properly prepared and know how to use the perfect phrase at the appropriate moment.

# Chapter 16
# Supporting a Proposal

You don't want to talk too much at meetings when you support the meeting's agenda and a proposal, but you always want to make a few pertinent comments to enhance your image. If you don't have a pertinent comment, then you are better off saying nothing at all. The key to making pertinent comments is to come to the meeting prepared. Before a meeting you should put together the following:

- A list of the major reasons for which you support the proposal
- Specific examples of past problems or successes that have led you to support this proposal
- Detailed examples of how this proposal would help your area of responsibility

## Asking Clarifying Questions

One reason for making a list of major reasons for supporting a proposal is that it guides you in asking clarifying questions that support the proposal and reinforce your reasons for supporting it. In most meetings the presenter and other members won't cover all of the key reasons for which you're supporting a proposal and you can bring out those points.

For example, if you're attending a meeting that proposes a new system for requesting quality control tests based on a customer request, you could ask the clarifying question, "How do you plan to monitor the response time to ensure it meets customers' expectations?" This clarifying question would enable the presenter to make a better case for the proposed system in terms of response time.

### QUESTIONS RELATED TO BENEFITS

You can reinforce the benefits of a proposal effectively with a clarifying question. Just be sure, before you ask the question, that the answer will support the proposal. In the example above, the clarifying question about response time would not be good if the response time with the new system would be longer. You can make your question more effective if you preface it with a brief statement about an issue that concerns you.

- Will your proposal impact our staffing problems in customer service?
- I've been looking for ways to justify the cost of adding new equipment in my department. Do you believe your proposed system will provide me the tools to do that?

## QUESTIONS RELATED TO CURRENT OR PAST PROBLEMS

The ideal way to add value to the discussion of a proposal you support is to give a specific example of a problem or situation in the past that the proposed action would resolve or avoid. State the example, with enough detail so the other participants remember the situation, and then ask how the proposed action would solve or prevent such problems.

- We had problems on the Santa Monica job in staging shipments at the right time. We couldn't get the right products delivered as needed for the installation. We also couldn't locate two products that were received three months before we needed them. Can you explain how this system would have prevented that problem?

- We had three small renovations of homes in Apple Valley where we fell behind schedule due to allocating staff to other projects. We didn't realize we were behind until one week before the completion date. How would your new proposed procedures prevent an occurrence similar to that?

## QUESTIONS RELATED TO MAJOR COMPANY GOALS

Managers and supervisors try to achieve the results expected of them while helping the organization achieve its goals. You will help the proposals you support gain approval if you can emphasize that they are helping to meet an organization goal. Avoid asking questions that are trite, such as "Will this program help achieve [company goal]?" Instead, you're better off stating the more specific goal of the proposed action and then asking if this is a shift in the organization's goals.

- Your proposal appears to focus on improving our response time to customers. Is this a shift from our goal of cutting overhead to 8 percent of sales this year? If not, how would the proposed action affect the 8 percent goal?
- The thrust of your program appears to be to streamline our testing procedures to cut production time by two days. Will this impact our organization goal to be more responsive to special order requests for new applications?

# Introducing Compelling Examples

To be compelling, examples must be specific and detailed. Anything less, and people will dismiss your comments and your examples might even weaken the position you are trying to support.

## EXAMPLES OF GOOD RESULTS FROM SIMILAR ACTIONS IN SIMILAR SITUATIONS

The situations don't have to be identical, just similar. Nothing succeeds like success, so organizations like to repeat actions that have been effective.

- There was a somewhat similar situation when we did the joint venture with [be specific]. Our two systems couldn't be coordinated at all and we outsourced the project of reentering data from [be specific] into our system. The approach worked well and the cost was much lower than if we'd tried to integrate the two systems ourselves.

- Two years ago we had a similar situation with [be specific]. We considered several options and decided to [specify action]. We had good results: the customer not only kept us as a supplier, but increased the size of its purchase order.

## EXAMPLES OF POOR RESULTS FROM OTHER ACTIONS

A strong case can be made for pursuing another proposed action if alternative actions in the past have failed.

- I think the last similar situation involving [be specific] is still vivid in everyone's mind. We tried out a different solution, [be specific], and the results were not good: using that solution set us back in our relationship with the vendor at least six months. I personally support trying this proposed action.

- I believe we all supported trying to [be specific] last year with [customer or prospect], who could have been a large customer. I think we all agree we overlooked the eventual negative reaction we faced. This proposal, at least as far as I can see, reduces any potential negative reaction and is our safest option.

## EXAMPLES OF SIMILAR ACTIONS THAT GAINED BROAD SUPPORT

Some action plans that a group develops gain broad support while others do not. Most groups would much rather choose action plans with broad support, as the support makes it easier to implement the plans and the group can avoid or at least reduce criticism.

- One strong aspect of this proposal is that it is similar to our response to [be specific]. We had support from the entire organization then, and I expect we can get it this time. That support will greatly reduce the time it takes us to implement this strategy.

- The feedback I'm hearing seems to indicate that we need to move quickly. I don't think we can do that without broad support through the company. Based on our experiences with [group 1] and [group 2] (be specific), I believe this proposal offers our best chance to get the support we need.

# Explaining How the Proposal Would Help You

The most compelling support you can offer is to show how the proposed action would benefit you, especially if that benefit might not be obvious to all the participants. But you want to express the benefit in terms of how the action proposed would help you do a better job for the organization, not as something that would just make your job easier.

## IMPROVING YOUR PERFORMANCE FOR KEY STAKEHOLDERS

How would the proposed action help you meet or exceed the expectations of key stakeholders such as customers, senior management, or your distribution network?

- We have a weekly conference call with [stakeholder] to address our current status of back orders. This report will give [stakeholder] instant access to our back orders and expected ship dates two to three weeks prior to the date, so we can shuffle production to meet customer emergencies.

- Currently our timing projections for incoming cash flow from receivables can be off by ten days to three or four weeks. We currently have one month of operating cash on hand, from our line of credit, due in part to our inability to project cash flow accurately. These proposed changes should cut our operating cash on hand by 60 percent, which will reduce the bank's concern that we're drawing too much on our line of credit.

**IMPROVING YOUR EFFICIENCY**

Being more efficient is important only if it allows you to take on additional responsibilities that help the organization, or if you can cut costs. So always tie an efficiency report to a benefit.

- The Investor Relations Department has been requesting more press releases on new products and significant market activities. If we bring in a new graphics department, we will be able to cut our time preparing those documents by 50 to 80 percent, which would allow us to do a better job on publicizing positive developments within the company.

- We have had to turn down custom orders from sales over the last two years, which often means we aren't doing the development work needed to grow sales. Adding this inventory planning system will allow us in three or four months to pull resources into a custom order department.

# Chapter 17
# Contesting a Proposal

In most meetings you will support proposals or be at least neutral. But there are times when you can't support a proposal for any number of reasons, including that it would negatively impact areas under your responsibility, it would load too much work onto you, or you feel the action is bad policy. Then you want to contest the proposal and try to change it—but you need to contest carefully, as you don't want to be perceived as negative or self-serving and you don't want to generate personal animosity toward you.

The key to contesting a proposal is not to attack it head on: stating that someone has made an error in facts and/or analysis won't help you look professional and won't make you any friends. Instead, you should take the tack that you have some additional information relevant to the issue and that this information may be important enough to warrant reevaluating the proposal.

# Clarifying the Premise Behind the Proposal

The premise is the basic underlying principle that is typically guiding a decision. In many meetings, the premises or the participants vary greatly, which leads to problems in discussing an issue and proposals.

For example, in a meeting about production forecasts, the participants might have these premises or priorities that govern their thinking:

- Production: smooth, orderly production rate without overtime
- Sales: meeting all customer orders within normal lead time
- Finance: highest gross margin for product produced
- General management: growing revenue while maintaining a reasonable margin
- Human resources: avoid burdening plant workers to minimize union problems

It's no wonder that meetings give rise to conflicts when participants have different starting points. The easiest way to derail a proposal is to challenge the premise behind the presenter's point of view. Start by getting the premise on the table.

## CLARIFYING A PREMISE AND ASKING ABOUT TIMING

I've never had much luck asking people to explain their premise. Instead I've found it more effective to state what seems to be their premise and ask if that is correct. It often works better to state the premise as a goal.

- I have a strong impression that your goal is to smooth out production and control costs more closely from product to product. I'm wondering if this is the right time for this proposal. We have a huge backlog of orders. Shouldn't reducing that backlog be a priority? This sounds like a proposal more appropriate for when our backlog is low.

- I agree with your goal of reducing the computer redundancy from our acquisition of Harland Industries. But shouldn't our goal be first to plan our operational strategy after merging before we worry about merging the two legacy computer systems?

## PRAISING THE PROPOSAL BUT CHALLENGING THE PREMISE

One way to maintain good working relationships is to be able to praise the proposal, but then challenge the premise. This way you are not challenging the presenter's reasoning, but just his or her starting point. This is not perceived as a great threat, since people typically base their thinking on premises most closely related to their job. For instance, production people have, as a premise, that they want smooth flow and they focus on that rather than a company goal of keeping lead time at seven days.

- I think your proposal would do a good job at keeping our training rooms utilized at a constant rate. But is that our real goal here? Shouldn't we schedule our training rooms in order to make training available to people when it suits their schedule.

- Your staffing proposal will keep our overtime down, which would appear to keep our costs down. But I'm worried it ignores that we might have times where people won't have any work to do. In those situations, the proposal could raise either the labor costs per part or our overhead levels. We need to balance both aspects and not worry only about overtime costs.

## FRAMING THE PREMISE UNFAVORABLY

You should use this tactic rarely, as some presenters or meeting leaders will take offense. But if the proposal would hurt you and the flow is not going your way, you may need to use this tactic on occasion. It's more likely to be effective if you use it infrequently.

- I'm getting the impression you want to set our quality standards based on the tests available with our current equipment. That seems like a self-serving approach. Shouldn't we be setting our tests based on the needs of our customers?

- From what I've heard so far, the new manufacturing management system seems to deliver everything accounting wants. But should that be our goal? Shouldn't the system cut delivery time and increase efficiency in the plant? That's a goal that will help the company grow.

## Introducing Concepts Overlooked in the Premise

Whenever you start with a premise or a goal in mind, it is inevitable that you will overlook considerations that concern people who start with different premises. An accounting-oriented production planning system, for example, will probably ignore a key consideration of sales: the ability to fast-track an order for a key customer.

### OVERLOOKED ACTIVE INITIATIVES

At any given time, in any organization, there are several initiatives under way and these initiatives can clash. I've found it useful to keep a copy of e-mails or memos that I've received with initiatives—just in case I need to find a reason to contest a proposal. Don't do this every time, but it can be smart now and then to preface your objection with a positive statement.

- I think there is a lot of merit to your proposal. But I'm concerned that it clashes with the [be specific] initiative from [be specific]. I think we might be developing a conflict situation with [describe issue] and, as a result, both of our proposals will fail.

- Before we get too far into this discussion, I just want to bring up an action proposal that was implemented by [be specific]. It covered [be specific]. I think we are better off finding a proposal that can work cooperatively with that proposal or by taking no action at all.

## OVERLOOKING KEY STAKEHOLDERS' NEEDS

Nobody wants to upset key stakeholders and it is often best to offer proposals that make the stakeholders happy. Don't use this strategy unless you can offer a specific example as evidence of what stakeholders want. Without specifics, you will be perceived to be just negative.

- I met with [key stakeholder] two weeks ago and he mentioned that he was hoping our group could provide more assistance to [be specific]. This proposal seems to be taking the opposite tack and I feel we risk alienating [stakeholder].

- Our two key customers, [name the customers], have hammered us relentlessly for small delays from our promised ship dates. If we focus resources on this new proposal, we won't have the resources to turn around our late shipment situation.

## OVERLOOKING KEY ORGANIZATIONAL GOALS

You won't have much problem killing a proposal that conflicts with organizational goals, but you can also make a case that a proposal that does not serve organizational goals will take away resources from proposals or plans that do.

- The plan for this year called for the organization to [be specific]. This proposal seems to be taking us in a different direction. I'm not sure we want to commit ourselves to a program that sooner or later is going to be viewed as off track by the rest of the organization.

- What concerns me is that we are considering moving forward with a proposal that doesn't meet any of the specific organizational goals for the year. Already we are several months into this year and we haven't taken a single action to support this year's priorities. I'm in favor of developing at least a short list of actions that would support our priorities before committing resources to this program.

## Explaining How the Proposal Would Hurt Your Performance

You must be careful when talking about how a proposal would affect your responsibilities, as people might perceive you as a whiner or uncooperative. But you must speak up and outline problems, you would face and the consequences of those problems or people will expect you to hit all of your performance goals. Your best approach is to frame your problems within a proactive strategy and hope people will see that the proposed action is disruptive or decide to provide you the assistance you need to overcome the problems you'll face.

### COMMENT POSITIVELY AND REQUEST HELP

Rather than say you don't have resources to complete the project, a reaction that could be perceived as negative, specify what help you would need if the proposal were approved.

■ I like this approach and I can see how it will help the company. But it would add a lot to my responsibilities. I would have to deal with several new customer issues, including [be specific]. I would be able to handle those issues if I turned over my duties regarding [be specific] to someone else or if someone shared his or her assistant with me.

■ I can see that this proposal has support from the group and I want to cooperate in any way I can to help the program succeed. But to do that I'm going to need some help to finish the [name of] project bid on time. I could assume new responsibilities if someone could help do the electrical design and the part lists and someone could go through the opening bid walkthrough.

## EXPLAIN HOW YOU COULD RESHUFFLE YOUR PRIORITIES

Again, you want to make these comments with a can-do attitude but still make it clear that the proposal would disrupt your activities.

- This proposal would create some challenges for me. It would [be specific]. I could respond to those challenges and help implement the program, but only if I canceled or delayed significantly the two new initiatives, [spell out initiatives], that I've taken on recently.

- I'm glad to help on this project, but in order to take the actions outlined here I'm going to have to make it my number-two priority. That means I'll have to back out of several other priorities, including [be specific]. I know those priorities are important to [stakeholder], so she will need an explanation in advance of why I won't hit the target dates for those priorities.

## USE THE PROPOSAL TO ADVANCE YOUR AGENDA

Often you have several action items on your agenda that you'd like to implement to make your efforts more productive. Sometimes those action items meet with resistance for various reasons. If you state that you can cooperate, but you will need help to implement your agenda, you will either help derail the proposal or be able to move ahead with your agenda items.

- I want to be a team player here, even though the proposal will impact me negatively in several ways, including [be specific]. I believe I can free up enough resources to overcome those negative effects if I can get the go-ahead to implement my proposal regarding [name it] that deals with [the situation]. If not, I'll have to sacrifice several other priorities to help out with this proposal.

- As I've been listening to the discussion, I've been trying to figure out how I can free up the resources needed. Without dropping any priorities that would upset other departments, I can participate if I can go ahead with the proposal I made last month on [name issue]. There was some resistance to that proposal, but it seems to me that overall it is a win-win situation for us all if I take on the responsibilities required of me by this new proposal and at the same time move ahead on the [name of] proposal.

# Chapter 18
# Adding Value to
# the Action Plan

If you want to show management potential and move up through the organization, this chapter is for you. The reality in most organizations is that promotions, especially to key positions, are done by a consensus of all the managers, based primarily upon their impressions of candidates. Performance reviews play a role, but there will be several candidates with strong performance reviews. Your immediate manager will know you well, but other managers will know you and your capabilities solely or primarily through observing you in meetings.

Fortunately, meetings present many opportunities for you to show your expertise—but only if you come to the meetings prepared to discuss the topics and be able to project your views in ways that show a team attitude.

# Opening a Plan up for Further Discussion

Upper-level managers judge your management potential both by how you can lead a group and by whether or not you are a team player. This is especially true for your first few promotions. These two criteria seem to be in conflict, and maybe they are, but you can be both a leader and a team player by taking a soft approach to putting your ideas forward so that the group will be willing to adopt them. Your supervisor will notice that the ideas are coming from you, and a team approach will help put your ideas into action.

## SUGGESTING A BROADER VISION OR GREATER SCOPE

The person who makes a proposal is generally not interested in thinking bigger, as his or her first reaction might be that doing so would just mean doing more work. So you need to suggest expanding the vision or scope as a way to make the proposed project actually easier.

- I'm concerned that this project won't make it onto the priority list of the departments we need help from, especially [department]. One suggestion to make sure you get the support you need might be to broaden the scope of the project to include [specify activity].
- I'm not sure you're representing enough impact to get approval to fund the proposal. One suggestion might be to expand the scope of the project to include increasing support for the international sales department, since the staff there constantly complains about our poor communication feedback time.

## OFFERING TO COORDINATE WITH OTHER PROPOSALS

Here again you need to focus not on the advantages of your suggestion, but rather on ways in which your proposal could help others implement their proposals.

- We may run into resistance with this program from the [be specific] group because they have a major initiative now to [be specific]. We might be able to get better results if we coordinate our proposal with their program. That way the two groups can help each other.

- We have two projects under way now that are running under the radar, [project 1] and [project 2]. This proposal could be a third. Wouldn't we be better off combining all three so that we have a project with high impact that people will notice?

## ADJUSTING THE PLAN FOR ORGANIZATIONAL OR KEY STAKEHOLDERS' GOALS

You always improve your chances of gaining acceptance of your ideas when your suggestions benefit the entire organization. Suggestions that involve key goals also show your supervisors that you have a broad perspective that will help you be an effective manager.

- One of the key organizational goals is to [be specific]. With just a few modifications to the proposal, including [state parts of proposal], I believe we would be right on target for that goal. That would help get the support we need to implement the project, as it would then have a higher profile.

- We may not be able to implement this project without support from the [name of] department and I'm not sure they will see this effort as having enough impact on our stakeholders' needs to give us full support. We could strengthen our position by making a few changes so that we meet the needs of [key stakeholder] as well as our own objectives.

## Sharing Ownership of Your Ideas

Even great supervisors and managers do best when they are considered team players; it is even more important for an up-and-comer in the organization. Don't worry about ownership of your ideas: even if you don't get credit for each of them, people will recognize your contributions if you consistently add value at meetings.

### STARTING WITH JUST A THOUGHT

You'll get a lot more support for your ideas if you simply get a discussion started on a topic, as a point of consideration, rather than jumping into suggestions or recommendations for changing a proposed course of action. Start by expressing a concern or a possibility for improving the proposal before offering any specific ideas.

- I had a glimmer of an idea about how we might be able to expand the vision of the program so it would be an easier sell to the rest of the organization. What we could do is [state actions], which, if I'm not mistaken, meets many of the organization's first six-month goals. If the group agrees, maybe we could spend ten minutes discussing this approach.

- A thought occurred to me that maybe we could get more money to support the program if we could find a way to show how this initiative would work with the manufacturing department's efforts to [state actions]. One way to do this might be to [state idea]. If this thought makes sense to all of you, maybe we could all work together to refine it so it can be presented to management.

**ASKING FOR INPUT**

- I'm not sure this solution would really work, but what we could do is [state actions]. Do you think this concept has merit? And if you do, do you have any ideas how we could maximize the benefits that we could get by taking this approach?

- There is something about this plan that makes me uneasy. The proposal would make it more difficult for certain customers to enter orders. Is there a way we can recast the proposal to eliminate that drawback?

# Presenting Your Addition as an Improvement

You usually can't attempt to substantially change a meeting proposal without causing hard feelings. Instead, you have to praise and support the proposal and then only add modifications that will be perceived as strengthening the plan. You can focus on better meeting the specific goals of the proposals, meeting organizational goals, and facilitating support throughout the organization.

All meeting proposals have two elements: achieving a specific goal and doing it within a certain time and with a certain amount of work and resources. So you can make suggestions to improve the goals of the project or to reduce the time, work, and/or resources needed to reach those goals. Your suggestions won't be popular if they just add too much work to the proposed plan, even if they would improve the results. The best proposal improvement is one in which you offer to do something to help make the project better without requiring that the presenter do additional work.

## HELPING ACHIEVE THE PROJECT GOALS

You should first reaffirm the goals and then offer help that significantly improves the project.

- The proposal seems to be on track for meeting the goal of [state goal]. One thing that I could do to support the project's goal and help this proposal is to [be specific]. If you agree that would help, why don't we include my action item with the proposal so the plan shows greater potential impact on the organization?

■ You might be able to significantly reduce your burden for this proposal if you could have the IT people change their [name of] report. They have been requesting that we drop some of our requirements. We could do that for the IT department and then have them add this new feature. Then our job would be much easier.

## HELPING TARGET ORGANIZATIONAL GOALS

Depending on your organization, this can be a very important point, or one not worth considering. If your company requires a quarterly or semiannual report from your group, organizational goals are important and anything you do that could help support those goals will help your group.

■ Without too much effort on our part, I think we could change the program slightly so that it would help achieve the organizational goal of [be specific]. We could further strengthen our support of the goal by coordinating it with my current project in ways that [be specific].

■ I have a few suggestions if we are interested in taking on a leading role in meeting the organizational goal of increased responsiveness to special customer requirements. We could add, without too much effort, another action item that would provide for storing and activating custom testing procedures to meet the requirements of our two biggest customers, [name customers].

## FACILITATING SUPPORT THROUGHOUT THE ORGANIZATION

Even though departments and groups within an organization may feud on occasion, a department or a group cannot succeed without support from other departments and groups. That means you have to be attentive to what helps other groups in your organization in order to make it easier to get cooperation from them in the future.

■ We owe the shipping group for rearranging the truck shipment to [location] when the order was changed just before shipment. We could help the people in shipping if we incorporated into this project their long-time request for better forecasting tools. That would allow us to meet our goal of simplifying the budgeting process, while converting the sales numbers into projected units and truckload shipments for the shipping department.

■ Could we use this proposal to also address our cash flow management problem? Right now people wait two to four weeks for a requisition to be approved. With just a few changes, this proposal could provide the departments with a schedule of their discretionary funds available for the next four to six weeks so they could set their own spending priorities.

# Chapter 19
# Handling Attacks and Adversaries

There will be many times when you will come under attack at a meeting. Sometimes you'll have done something wrong, sometimes you'll be a scapegoat, and sometimes it won't be clear why you're being attacked.

The first step when under attack is to stay cool and not panic. Unless the attacker is a superior, he or she usually looks worse than the victim. But no matter what the circumstances, even when you have committed a bad error, you can still survive.

One point to remember is that making a mistake is not that negative if it's a result of some actions that you have taken. A good number of your decisions and actions might not turn out well, so it's important to accept mistakes as normal, deal with the consequences and criticism, and keep your attitude positive. There is no point in trying to prove that the person attacking you is wrong. That can only make you seem argumentative and difficult.

# Keeping Your First Response Positive

Of course the natural desire is to either defend yourself or lash out against your attacker. But that won't get you far and it won't help your image as an up-and-comer in the organization. So the first step is to count to 10 or 15: a brief pause helps you relax and collect your thoughts. It also lets people know you are annoyed by the attack. Then, when you respond, start on a positive note.

## RESPONDING TO PETTY OR PERSONAL ATTACKS

Such an attack may come, for example, because someone is taking your comments as criticism of him or her, someone who dislikes you, or someone feels you're rising too fast in the organization. Acknowledge the attack briefly, but then concentrate on the importance of the goal.

- I'm somewhat disturbed that you feel that way, but the real issue here today is how we can develop an action plan to address an important problem [state problem]. I'd rather not get into a blame game here as I don't see how it would keep the meeting moving forward.

- I agree we are not getting the results that the group and I have gotten in the past. I think we can all point the finger at each other, but that's not going to help anyone. There are many issues that each of us face daily that may be interfering with our results. What we really need to do is focus on what we can do to improve our results.

## RESPONDING TO ATTACKS DUE TO TURF BATTLES

These are one of the most frequent sources of attack. People tend to be very sensitive to losing authority and responsibilities. Inevitably new proposals and action plans challenge the established order and people will often respond by attacking whoever is encroaching on their turf. The attack against you is not personal, but a reaction to a loss of power. In this situation, a strong response is to acknowledge the person's feelings, but then state how the change improves his or her position.

- I understand that this topic seems to threaten your responsibilities over certain functions in the organization. (It is more effective to be specific.) Change is coming and we are all going to be affected in one way or another. Maybe we can work together to figure out how you can step forward and take on new responsibilities that will maintain your scope of authority.

- I know you are upset because you think I'm cutting into your area of authority. I'm not trying to do that. I'm trying to readjust how we respond to the changes in the organization so our group can take a leading role. Let's all be open to discussing the possibilities and let's see where that takes us. I'm hoping we can work things out so we can contribute more to the organization, not less.

## RESPONDING TO ATTACKS THAT REVEAL HOSTILITY

For example, someone may be attacking your efforts in order to shift attention away from his or her poor performance, or maybe your proposal makes some changes that they fear and oppose. People often panic when they feel, believe, or know that their own situation is being questioned or changed; when that happens, they may lash out rather than discuss the situation rationally. Your best bet here is to be positive and then ask for the underlying cause of the hostility.

- I believe we have always had a good working relationship and I'm confident your remarks were not a personal attack. I wonder if you're reacting to something other than the issue we're discussing. If you share the reason, maybe we can address your concerns.

- You seem to be reacting very negatively to the proposal to [be specific]. If you outline your concerns, I think all of us here will be willing to work with you to mitigate your concerns.

## Accepting the Blame

Everyone operates in a busy world with too much to do. Often, you will not get everything done that you intended. Just making excuses doesn't get you much respect. I found it is much more effective to first accept blame, at least partially, and then state what caused the delay and what you would like to do to rectify the situation.

### WHEN YOU ARE ALMOST EXCLUSIVELY AT FAULT

One reason meetings bog down is that participants spend so much time trying to deny responsibility for problems. One thing I learned long ago is to accept blame; then what can anyone else say? Afterwards, things will start to move along. If you are at fault, trying to find an excuse won't change that fact or fool anyone, so you might as well admit your error.

- I feel totally responsible for the situation. I know this was an important issue to several of you here and you were counting on me. I was pulled into another project for senior management that I didn't expect, but I still should have done better or, at the very least, I should have let you all know I wouldn't be able to meet my commitment. I've finished the other project now and I can devote time to meeting these objectives. I'd like another chance to rectify the situation. I promise I'll keep up to the new timetable.

- I know everyone is upset with me. Before the meeting breaks down, let me admit I was at fault and followed a course of action that jeopardized this entire project. I thought I could resolve our backorder situation by going to a quota system, but—as you all know—this decision backfired badly. I should have asked for advice from the group, but I failed to do that. I'm willing to take whatever action the group ends up recommending to try to salvage our situation.

## WHEN OTHERS ARE ALSO AT FAULT

Sometimes you will not be totally responsible for a problem. Usually in such situations you can deal with attacks by just pointing out that there is not just one person to blame and that the meeting will go nowhere if the participants pass responsibility around the table. Instead, it's smartest to just move forward.

- Look, even though we don't want to admit it, I think we all know there's plenty of blame to go around. Rather than trying to pin someone unfairly with responsibility for where we are today, let's focus instead on figuring out how we are going to turn the situation around. Once we move forward, I think we will all forget about blaming anyone.

- I know everyone would like to blame someone else, but I think this is a situation where we all have fallen down in one way or the other. Rather than spend all our energy in a negative direction, either defending ourselves or attacking others, let's concentrate instead on figuring out a plan to get back on track.

# Being Willing to Consider Other Solutions

Sometimes the attacks keep coming despite your initial efforts. That persistence may make you really feel like lashing back, but that again is not the course of action to take. You want to remember now that people of action, those who move the organization forward, rarely keep criticizing; they know from experience how easy it is to make a mistake. The people who won't stop criticizing are those who sit on the sidelines and think their job is to criticize others. The way to turn these people around is to be willing to adopt their suggestions and then make it clear the action you are following is theirs. That often scares the critics off, as they will fear that criticism could later be directed at them if their proposal is followed.

Two traits you don't want to exhibit when under attack are being stubborn and being too proud to accept input or advice from others. That's counterproductive: the meeting typically won't reach any resolution, and such behavior will not improve your image as a competent candidate for greater responsibilities.

## WHEN ATTACKS CONTINUE FROM ONE PERSON

Frequently you can reverse the attacker simply by asking for his or her solution and then stating you will implement it. The person is most likely to back off immediately; if not, and the other participants do not criticize the solution suggested, you might want to see if it works.

- [Name], since you have been pecking away at me here for most of the meeting, I feel you must have a solution that I haven't found. Obviously I've struggled here, so why don't you tell me what steps you feel I should take? Then, unless the others here have strong objections to your plan, I'll give it a try.

■ Obviously nothing I've done or proposed has met with your satisfaction. Do you have another course of action you'd like me to try? I'm willing to consider another approach. I think one of the reasons you've been so adamant in your attacks is that you have an alternative solution to propose.

## WHEN THE GROUP SEEMS TO BE AGAINST YOU

The situation is more difficult when the group seems to be swaying against you. Being combative isn't going to help here. Looking for another solution might not work well here, either, as the group might just roll you out of the discussion. Instead, you want to acknowledge that you and the group are not in sync, possibly because you're operating on a different premise or because you see the situation in a different light. For example, you might think that your problems have been caused by a poor vendor performance, while the others might feel that the customer's quality control department has unrealistic expectations. By focusing on the underlying assumptions, you might find that you and the group really are on different pages or you'll at least be restarting the conversation on a more positive note.

■ I feel like I'm totally out of sync with the group and that somehow I'm looking at the problem in a radically different way than the rest of you. If you don't mind, I'd like to go back and review what I feel we are trying to accomplish with this effort. Then I'd like to list the people and companies that are impacting the situation and identify each as a good or bad actor in this situation. One problem I'm sensing is that I have a different view from most of you on what brought this situation to a head.

- I'm apparently on a totally different page than everyone else. No one seems to understand the points I'm trying to make and I don't understand the points most of you are making. I'm hoping that we might have differences in our underlying reference points that are causing this misunderstanding. I have a list of a half-dozen reference points I'm using to analyze this situation. Let me read them to you so we can determine if we at least are starting our analysis from the same point.

# Chapter 20
# Committing to What You Can Deliver

Meetings often discuss proposals and action plans that can add to your duties and responsibilities. While you always want to project a can-do image, you have only so much time and you don't want to make commitments that you can't keep. This is a delicate balance: you need to take on more responsibilities for the good of the organization and your career, but not getting projects done or not adequately fulfilling your normal job responsibilities will reflect badly on you. So you need to guard your time and commitments without seeming like a whiner. Many people, when facing an overload of responsibilities, respond poorly, lashing out at others and becoming overly negative or uncommunicative. Being able to professionally avoid commitments you can't handle properly can be challenging, but it is a skill you need in order to move ahead in the organization.

You want to be viewed as someone who is trying to make things happen, so you want to do the following:

- Support the merits of the plan.
- Express a strong desire to help implement the plan.
- Explain why you don't have the time to commit to the effort involved.
- Suggest accommodations in your current workload that would allow you to act.

## Acknowledging the Merits of a Plan

When you start to sense you are going to be overloaded with a commitment, the natural tendency is to attack the plan. From that point on in the discussion, you will be viewed as an obstructionist. So you want to start with a positive response to the plan and express support.

### WHEN YOU ARE A MAJOR PLAYER IN THE PLAN

In some cases you will have to do most of the work required in an action plan. If you fail to act, that may kill the program and upset people. If you can't meet the commitments, you must avoid looking uncooperative, so you need to be careful to respond as positively as possible.

- There are many points of this program that I feel positive about. It will clearly help both the customers and the production planning group avoid long lead times. I can clearly see the value, both for myself in terms of my responsibilities and for [other party to benefit], and I definitely want to do what I can to help.

- This is great. I've often thought about a program similar to this, but I never worked through all the coordination required from all the other groups. I see the same benefits of the program as you and I realize that we have a window of opportunity here where we can do a lot to solve this recurring problem.

### WHEN YOUR ROLE SUPPORTS OTHERS

You are in not nearly as much danger when you are supporting other people or departments that will be responsible for the major actions of a plan. If you convince people that you can't meet the commitment, often others will pick up the responsibilities that would have been assigned to you. So your support can be more subdued: often just one or two sentences is best.

- It looks like you've put a lot of effort into this proposal and I certainly support your program goals.
- You're offering a creative approach here, and there is something to be said for changing direction when a program has gone stale. I favor looking at this proposal and seeing if we can move ahead with implementation.

## Expressing Concern About Your Commitment Level

You must always guard against being categorized as difficult. Once you are labeled "difficult," you will have a tough time restoring your image. It's equally bad to be perceived as someone who can't follow through on commitments. People should not be surprised if you express a concern about your commitment level; most supervisors or managers will expect you to think through your time allocation before committing. You don't need to feel defensive or on the spot; just state your case with a few facts to support it.

### TIME CONSTRAINTS BECAUSE OF OTHER COMMITMENTS

You might need four to six months to really understand how much time a new initiative requires of you. Projects can cause you to become severely overcommitted, if not immediately or soon, at least after two or three months. Generally, if you mention the other new programs to which you're committed, people will try to work out an arrangement with you to reduce new commitments.

- My main problem in being able to commit to this new project is the responsibilities I accepted recently for the [be specific] initiative at the request of [person]. I've just started that project and right now the time required isn't too extensive, but I believe that in just a few months I could have a very heavy time burden that would make a large commitment to this project impossible.

- I know this project is important, but I was given a project to work with customer service and accounting to reconfigure our invoice system to better reflect the discounts we offer. I'm worried that I won't be able to do justice to either project if I try to do both.

## TIME CONSTRAINTS BECAUSE OF A LACK OF SUPPORT IN OTHER AREAS

You might have had to pick up additional duties because someone has left your organization or because another group in the company is shorthanded. One way to broach the subject is to ask about the timing: how critical is an immediate start? That implies you have a resource problem, while still conveying a desire to help out. Another approach is to find out if any people in charge of the other projects to which you're committed would allow you to delay that work so you can accept and meet this new commitment.

- Is there any chance the project could be delayed for 60 days? I have a problem in my group right now because we're picking up workload from the [name of] Division. This additional responsibility has taken all my time. They are supposed to correct the situation in about 60 days. I'm enthusiastic about helping out with this program, which I support 100 percent, but I need a delay or I just won't be able to help.

- I can meet this commitment and help out, but only at the expense of dropping my support to the quality control team. Otherwise, I don't have time. If we can't drop the production team, I have five other major activities that consume most of my time. If I could offload one of those projects, I'd be able to help.

## TIME CONSTRAINTS BECAUSE YOU NEED MORE RESOURCES

You can't use the excuse of not having enough resources in every situation or you'll be seen as negative or as an obstructionist, but there are times when it's necessary.

- Right now, without the right software program, I'd need to commit 60 percent of my time to meet my commitments for this proposal. In July, with a new budget, I can get this program and then meet your needs with just 10 percent of my time. I'm just not in a position to take on anything more right now.

- As you know, our group has lost two people and we have all stopped doing anything except the highest-priority projects. I don't know what project I can drop to do this. I can ask my supervisor about dropping projects to do this, but I can't guarantee that she will agree to drop any of them.

## Stating What You Need

You love the proposal and would love to be able to get involved in it, but you have constraints that prevent you from doing that. The last step to cement your can-do, up-and-coming positive attitude is to state exactly what you would need to be able to live up to the commitments people want from you. You just need to be sure that what you need is reasonable and that you will be able to deliver on your commitment if you get what you ask for. In the first two sections of this chapter, I've advised hinting at the resources you need. Here you must be specific in asking for what you want. You may not know the specific details on the spot. If not, ask if you can prepare a follow-up memo or e-mail detailing what you would need to live up to the commitment.

### ASKING TO OFFLOAD WORK

Even if you will be submitting a detailed list of what you need, you still should offer enough of a list at the meeting so that people don't think you're just resisting the proposal. I've found that it is wise to prepare a list of your major projects to bring to any meeting when you sense that new responsibilities may come your way.

■ I'm willing to help out on this project, provided I can offload one of my other projects. I have three projects that I could drop that would free up enough time. They are [project 1] , [project 2], and [project 3]. Each project takes about three to four hours per week. I can put together a

more detailed list in the next couple of days that I can
e-mail to each of you.

■ I need a little help here. I understand that this new project is
quite important and I'm willing to do my part, but I'm going
to have to reduce or eliminate some of the work I'm doing
now and I'm not sure how to prioritize the tasks. I'll need to
contact the people who are counting on my work on their
projects and let them know what will happen. Here's a list of
the four main tasks I do, along with the people who count
on me to do those tasks. Which of these projects do you
think I can scale back or transfer to someone else?

## ASKING FOR ADDITIONAL RESOURCES

Personally I prefer asking for additional resources rather than
offloading projects. Managers realize that new initiatives take
more effort and other resources, so they should not be upset
if you ask for more resources, as long as your request is reasonable. If they turn you down, then you can ask to offload
projects or tasks.

■ I've been just looking at my time and my group's time, trying to find a way to take on this project. I can do this
either by bringing on a part-time administrative person or
by switching to a new computer program that would cut
the time of doing [be specific] by [state percent] percent.
The cost of a part-time administrative person would be
$28,000 per year and the cost of implementing the com-
puter program would be $8,000 for two licenses.

■ I can reduce the back orders, but either I'll need to buy two
more pieces of injection molding equipment and find
another 5,000 square feet of factory, or we'll need to

replace our equipment. I recommend replacing the equipment: it would increase productivity, and I could meet this commitment without adding staff.

## About the Author

**Don Debelak** has a wide range of experience with over 30 years of meeting with big and small companies, with startups and established companies, and in positions from entry-level salesperson to president. The most constructive time has been as a marketing consultant: Debelak often attended or conducted two or three meetings a week, and every meeting needed a positive outcome in order to keep the projects moving forward.

Don Debelak was the monthly columnist of Bright Ideas for *Entrepreneur* magazine from 1999 to 2005 and is the author 12 books including *Perfect Phrases for Business Proposal and Business Plans* (McGraw-Hill, September 2005), *Business Models Made Easy* (Entrepreneur Media, Oct 2006), *Bringing Your Product to Market in Less Than a Year: Fast Track Approaches for Cashing in on Your Great Idea* (Wiley, 2nd edition, June 2005), and *Streetwise Marketing Plan* (Adams Media, 2000). He has been interviewed on national radio shows and Internet shows, and he has been featured in leading newspapers, including *The Wall Street Journal* and *The Washington Post*.

His Web site, **www.dondebelak.com**, offers assistance to companies introducing new products and offers business marketing advice for established companies.

# PERFECT PHRASES
## *for...*